MY FABULOUS
FASCIST
SUMMER VACATION

Brian Gruber

MY FABULOUS FASCIST SUMMER VACATION

A Journey Through Europe's Hearts of Darkness

My Fabulous Fascist Summer Vacation
Authored by Brian Gruber
ISBN: 9798340723451

PUBLISHED BY
Electric Memories Publishing
electric-memories.com

PRODUCERS
Lou Borrelli
Bill O'Luanaigh

EDITOR
Tom Vater

EDITORIAL CONTRIBUTORS
Charlie Evans
Jamie Wrate
Nicole Maron

DESIGNER
Alexandru Oprescu

COVER PHOTOGRAPHS, FROM LEFT TO RIGHT

António de Oliveira Salazar – Source: Archives of Alfredo Pereira de Lima.
Francisco Franco – Source: Biblioteca Virtual de Defensa Retrato Fotográfico Del Generalísimo D. Francisco Franco Bahamonde (MUE-120279), Public Domain.
Adolf Hitler – Source: Wikimedia.org, Mussolini and Hitler (c.1940), Public Domain.
Benito Mussolini – Source: Wikimedia.org, Mussolini and Hitler (c.1940), Public Domain.
Recep Tayyip Erdoğan – Source: U.S. Department of State, public domain per 17 U.S.C. § 101 and § 105 and the Department Copyright Information.
Viktor Orbán – Source: Gov.pl, Creative Commons Attribution 3.0 Poland license.
Donald Trump – Source: Gage Skidmore, flickr.com, Creative Commons Attribution-Share Alike 2.0 Generic license.

Contents

PROLOGUE ix

PREFACE xv

PORTUGAL: EUROPE'S LONGEST DICTATORSHIP 1

Aida Rechena • *Resistance and Freedom.* 2

Robert Paxton • *Authoritarian Nationalism* 13

Rui Carvalheira • *Lusotropicalism and the Sermon of the Fishes* 20

SPAIN: FRANCO KILLS THE REPUBLIC 41

Adam Hochschild • *The Global Battleground* 48

Carlos Sardiña Galache • *A Cult of Violence.* 51

Nick Lloyd • *Walking Barcelona* 56

FRANCE: MARSEILLE LAYOVER 63

Hazem El Moukaddem • *"I think we are on the edge."* 63

ITALY: MUSSOLINI'S LEGACY. 77

Paolo, Massimo, and Antonio • *The Pasta and Prosecco Summit.* . . . 87

Nick Carmody • *Tribalism and Personality Cults.* 105

GERMANY: HITLER WAS ELECTED 113

Bettina Sellers • *The Good Uncle* 115

Markus Naegele • *A Walk Through NS-Dokumentationszentrum* . . 123

Ingar Solty • *Maintaining the Facade* 134

Patrick Vater • *Advertising, Propaganda, and the Decline of Political Education* 138

AUSTRIA: VIENNA LAYOVER 145
   Gerhard Oberschlick • *You Have to Fight* 145
   Maria H. • *The Pharmacist's Daughter.* 150

HUNGARY: ORBÁN'S ILLIBERAL DEMOCRACY 159
   Peter Bakonyi • *A Culture of Identity* 159
   Miklos Martin-Kovacs • *Goulash Authoritarianism* 167
   Eric Alterman • *The Fight for Liberalism* 180

ROMANIA: CEAUSESCU AND COMING TO AMERICA 191
   Alexandru Oprescu • *Looking to America* 194

TURKEY: ERDOGAN AND THE JOURNEY'S END 209
   Danny Garcia • *An Homage to Atatürk* 210
   Asya • *The Flower of Resistance.* 214

ACKNOWLEDGEMENTS 220
ABOUT THE AUTHOR 222

*To Claire Gruber, Bernice Schwartz,
Yetta Rothenberg, Ruth Shapiro,
Mickey Greenberg, Ruth Alterman and
the multitudes of Jewish American women
whose grit, humor, and generosity of spirit
helped build this country.*

Prologue

The horror leaks into my body as I float between resistance to and full embrace of the moment. I want to open my heart and mind, to empathize, to feel. But the scale of the cruelty and terror is too much, so the body shudders.

The rage and astonishment overwhelm my sense of balance. The grief enters my viscera and I can no longer manage it. I start to weep openly. Embarrassed, I turn away from the other visitors. It was here that the prisoners were cremated after being murdered by asphyxiation in the nearby gas chambers. I am standing in front of one the ovens. The accounts on the walls detail the intentional cruelty of the camp guards and officers. The soldiers who liberated the camp, many of them Americans, were overwhelmed with disgust and grief when they arrived here in April 1945. They forced the local residents to enter the camp and view the crematorium, to see what they had allowed to happen, had even cheered on, all those years. There were piles of corpses, an estimated 3,000. There are photos of the dead on the walls, emaciated, skin and bones. Members of the NSDAP (Nazi party) were required to assist in burying the dead.

Most said they didn't know. Of course they knew.

Concentration camps, forced gatherings of people stripped of their rights and humanity, have been used by colonizers for centuries. The U.S., the country I was born in, rounded up, murdered, and isolated native Americans, contained African slaves in ships and market pens, and more recently put asylum seekers in cages, separating thousands from their children, intentionally, sometimes permanently. Each outrage is different—gas chambers were a German innovation—but the similarities are what instructs us. Humiliation, incarceration, cruelty, brutality, murder. Dachau was an early model, converted from a munitions factory in 1932, a place where the Germans experimented with all manners of torment. If you thought differently, you were sent here. If you dared to dissent, you were sent here. If you were considered subhuman due to race or nationality, you were sent here, though the early occupants were political opponents rather than Jews.

My emotional immersion in this monstrosity began with a visit to Munich's Nazi Documentation Center. I admire the Germans for trying to face what they or their forebears have done. Each floor pulled you in further. WWI, the 20s, the 30s, Kristallnacht, the camps, the slaughter, all expertly documented. What overwhelms me is the curation of the personal stories. Esteemed Jewish citizens paraded through the streets, humiliated, stripped of assets, then shipped off for extermination. I saw a photo of Jewish, Russian, and German inmates on a rainy street on April 26, 1945, in striped prison clothes and blankets, despondent, desperate, hopeless. SS officers forced some 8,900 to march through the communities of Allach, Pasing, and Gauting from the Dachau camp to certain death. Exhausted prisoners dropped dead along the road or were shot. The caption shook me. 'Many Germans who witnessed these death marches reacted with indifference and fear. Very few people tried to help the prisoners.'

And you and I, when do we become versed in the art of indifference?

The final months before the camp's liberation saw a catastrophic overflow of inmates. Thousands died in 'evacuation transports'. The photos throughout the camp bring the violence from the mythic and abstract to the physical and personal. How to fully grasp datapoints like six million Jewish dead, 2.7 million in gas chambers, two million in mass shootings and related massacres, one million in ghettos, labor camps, from disease and privation, 3.3 million Soviet POWs, 1.8 million non-Jewish ethnic Poles, a quarter million Romani, 300,000 Serbs, 300,000 people with disabilities? The numbers are estimates, rounded up.

The camp exhibits tell the stories of individual victims, Jews, communists, union organizers, student dissenters, intellectuals, Germans who chose something other than indifference. I try to study each of the hundreds of faces in the photos, a momentary act of empathy for those to whom the images bear witness. Some of the photos were taken illegally, others are documents of record-keeping-obsessed Nazi overlords, similar to the obsessive facial photo-taking of the Khmer Rouge, as they humiliated Cambodians forced to confess while being tortured, when they had nothing to confess, before they were beaten to death and buried in the killing fields.

Upon arrival, the men—all of the photos are of male inmates—wear tailored suits and walk with dignity, if not resignation. Do they know what's coming? I walk through the barracks, some reconstructed, and survey the photos of the guys crammed into unthinkable conditions.

A plaque honors the 42nd Rainbow Division and other U.S. Army units who liberated the camp on April 29, 1945 'in everlasting memory of the victims of Nazi barbarism'.

The camp gate is a replica. I restrain myself when a couple takes a selfie under the sign, smiling broadly. The SS had prisoners forge the inscription, 'Arbeit macht frei', or, 'Work sets you free'. Besides the morbid absurdity of the claim, it was a ruse to suggest to incoming prisoners that it was purely a labor and re-education camp, not a facility for mass murder.

An illegal photo taken somehow by Belgian prisoner Jean Brichaux shows the crematorium at work in the summer of 1944, gray smoke billowing from the chimney.

The schemata for the industrial killing machines is displayed. Someone drew these and planned the efficient movement of thousands through the process. There is a disinfecting chamber used for cleaning clothing stripped from victims. A photo of a massive pile of clothes outside the chamber, taken sometime in 1945 is displayed. A 'waiting room' where victims are informed on the use of the supposed 'showers'. By then, surely, it must have been common knowledge that friends who were marched away to those showers never returned. Standing in this 'waiting room', I look out of the same windows that thousands looked out before their horrible communal deaths. There is a radiator, two windows, a door on each side. Each prisoner who entered left behind their own stories, aspirations, histories, familial connections.

In the gas chambers, up to 150 at a time suffocated to death over a period of 15 to 20 minutes from the Zyklon B gas. After being murdered, the corpses were taken to 'death chambers' before they were cremated. The crematorium has four ovens, one on each side and two adjacent units in the center of the room. Millions were killed here.

The camp was built for a maximum of 6,240. Following the November pogrom in 1938, more than 11,000 Jews were arrested and transported to the already overcrowded camp. The number of prisoners rose to around 30,000 in late 1944. In some blocks, the SS crammed more than 2,000. When a typhoid epidemic broke out in November 1944, the barracks were set aside for quarantine, 'places of dying.'"

From prisoner testimonies posted in the barracks:

> *"The places for sleeping were now far too few… The beds had been pushed extremely close together…*

One slept with his head at the headboard, while the other's head was at the bottom of the bed."

"I do not know if the reader can imagine what it means when nearly 250 straw mattresses, most of them torn, just as many head rests, and 500 blankets, not to mention meager belongings ... are lying in a tumble in the dirt and rain."

Ashes of the cremated bodies were shoveled into pits, marked as graves after the liberation, with memorial plaques installed later. 'Grave of Thousands Unknown', one memorial announces. There is also a killing ground for executions, carried out through shots in the back of the neck against an earthen wall or in ditches. One memorial is a mound of rich green foliage headed by a tombstone topped by a large Star of David, further topped by a menorah. There is a slate with words in German, Hebrew, and English.

DO NOT FORGET.

We get the impression from newsreels of Nazi thugs beating Jews in the streets, from the totalitarian violence of the 1930s and 40s, that Adolf Hitler came to power violently. But no. Hitler was elected. And as the vulgarity, threats of violence, antidemocratic behaviors, and cruelty to ethnic minorities grew, Germans allowed it. Good church-going, children- and pet-loving, educated, cultured Germans allowed it, much as good churchgoing, children- and pet-loving, educated, cultured Americans allowed slavery, Reconstruction, native genocide, Jim Crow, and the carpet bombing of Vietnam, Cambodia, and Laos. The violent language and intentions become normalized, citizens are busy and thus indifferent, until one day one finds that a Hitler beer hall putsch or a January 6 assault on the United States Capitol are no big thing.

Hitler did time for his attempt at sedition, but he was released from prison after a few months, a few short years before he turned Germany into a fascist nightmare.

General Dwight D. Eisenhower knew it was essential to document the full brutality of fascist violence because, over time, people were likely to forget. Holocaust deniers, racists and white supremacists insist that the results of intolerance be obscured, diluted, normalized.

The soldiers, survivors, and relatives who saw the carnage firsthand suggest something different.

Preface

The world is sliding into a new era of autocracy and oligarchy. Few seem to care.

The United States, while always flawed, and all too frequently a supporter of autocracy, has also been a beacon of liberal democracy to many. Today, many advocates of people's governance and human rights see the U.S. as abandoning its constitutional convictions.

We have a problem with definitions. What is fascism? How do fascists ascend and take power? What are its human costs? And what can Americans and others learn from the countries that have embraced autocracy in the last century.

After globetrotting explorations of the aftereffects of U.S. military interventions and of models for successful citizen movements, I traveled the breadth of Europe to explore answers to those questions. Beginning on Lisbon's Atlantic coast and completing the journey at the Bosporus Strait in Istanbul I interviewed historians, activists, journalists, artists, and people on the street to understand why their countries chose authoritarian governments.

The Europe trip was scheduled for May. But a necessary bit of preventive surgery occupied me for three months, pushing the project to July.

My doctor suggested the removal of a tiny unwelcome bit of cellular material in something called a diverticulum. He told me that if the now small, contained cluster of cancer cells entered my bloodstream over the years, that would not be curable.

There is too much hyperbole in politics. But to me, the timely removal of this prospective poison in my body mirrored the state of the political health of my country. Trump's first term was a disaster. His only significant legislative achievement, in his first year, was a trillion-dollar tax cut targeted at wealthy donors. His incompetent handling of the COVID pandemic caused more unnecessary deaths than all American fatalities from wars, terrorist incidents, mass shootings, and epidemics in my lifetime. He degraded public discourse with crass, vulgar, often racist and misogynist outbursts. He made the United States a laughingstock overseas. He tried to stage a coup to block the results of the 2020 election, results validated by more than 60 courts, his election security team, state legislatures, and his own Attorney General.

But he was removed. I believe a second term would be disastrous for the country and the world as his fascistic threats and intentions permanently poison American democracy. That's my view. I traveled to Europe to get the unique perspectives of many others outside the echo chamber of U.S. media and politics.

The book is completed in time for an October press tour of the U.S. from New York to San Francisco, promoting in crucial "swing states" that will determine the presidential election. The intent is to sound the alarm about the creeping fascism of the Trump rightist movement and to get lovers of liberal democracy out to vote in November.

It was an extraordinary adventure, marked by many kindnesses, and memorable encounters. I hope you enjoy the ride.

BRIAN GRUBER
Koh Phangan, Thailand
September 22, 2024

---

* *During my visit to Dachau on July 21, U.S. President Joe Biden ended his re-election campaign and endorsed his Vice President Kamala Harris. Several interviews were conducted prior to this event.*

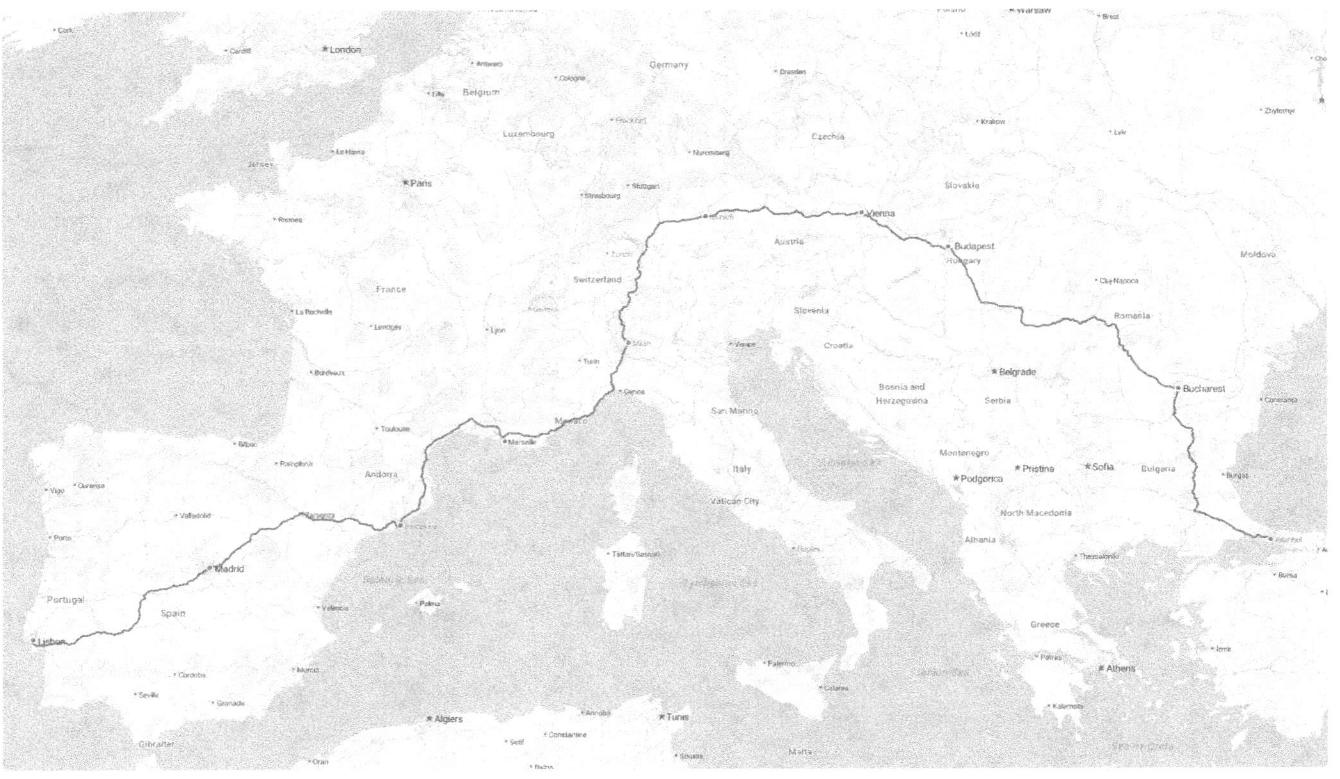

Cork
Cardiff
London
Antwerp
Cologne
Germany
Dresden
Poland
Warsaw
Brest
Łódź
Belgium
Lille
Luxembourg
Frankfurt
Nuremberg
Czechia
Kraków
Lviv
Le Havre
Jersey
Paris
Strasbourg
Stuttgart
Slovakia
Rennes
France
Zurich
Switzerland
Austria
Vienna
Budapest
Hungary
Cluj-Napoca
Moldova
La Rochelle
Limoges
Lyon
Milan
Slovenia
Romania
Bordeaux
Turin
Venice
Croatia
Belgrade
Bucharest
Genoa
San Marino
Bosnia and Herzegovina
Serbia
Constanța
Toulouse
Monaco
Marseille
Montenegro
Pristina
Sofia
Bulgaria
Bilbao
Andorra
Italy
Podgorica
Burgas
Pamplona
Vatican City
North Macedonia
Vigo
Ourense
Valladolid
Zaragoza
Barcelona
Albania
Thessaloniki
Porto
Tátari/Sassari
Naples
İstanbul
Madrid
Bursa
Portugal
Spain
Valencia
Palma
Greece
İzmir
Lisbon
Palermo
Patras
Athens
Córdoba
Murcia
Catania
Sevilla
Granada
Kalamata
Algiers
Annaba
Tunis
Gibraltar
Sétif
Constantine
Sousse
Malta
Oran
Biskra

CHAPTER 1

PORTUGAL

Europe's Longest Dictatorship

Whereupon the trip commences on the Atlantic coast with a bus trip to the Peniche fortress… an interview with preeminent U.S. fascism expert Dr. Robert Paxton… a walking tour through Portuguese history with Rui at Belem's Jeronimos Monastery.

It's Independence Day in the United States. Independence from centuries of kings, feudal lords, plutocrats, hoarders of wealth and power insisting on more wealth and power. Independence secured and enforced via a government of, by, and for the people, with separation of powers, an independent judiciary, the rule of law, free and fair elections, the right to assemble and protest, the freedom to speak and worship, with an unfettered assertive press.

The Etihad Airways flight arrives in Lisbon's Humberto Delgado airport from Bangkok via Abu Dhabi at 7:20am and, after a brisk push through immigration, I am in the airport's main area. Delgado was a brash Air Force general who tried to press his case in an election during the regime of longtime dictator António de Oliveira Salazar. By all accounts, Delgado won but, through voter suppression by an autocrat who refused to leave office peaceably, he was declared the loser. He was murdered for his trouble.

Sleep-deprived but adrenaline-soaked, dragging an Osprey Sojourn 60-liter roller backpack while shouldering an Osprey Nebula daypack, I have four hours before the bus to Peniche to take care of business: 1) a bathroom refresh and clothing change; 2) a purchase of a Euro-wide eSIM card for my iPhone 13 Pro Max; 3) locating with 1,000 percent certainty the FlixBus boarding spot; and 4) enjoying a Portuguese breakfast.

The Vodaphone rep informs me that I *CAN* take advantage of their 25-euro, 25 GB special but CANNOT effectively provision myself for the rest of my trip. I'll improvise on the road. The café options are modest but one seems busy so I drag my bags there and load up on pastels and espressos, feeling refreshed with my wardrobe change and new Lisbon phone number.

AIDA RECHENA
Resistance and Freedom

Aida Rechena, Director of the National Museum of Resistance and Freedom is available for an interview and the 16th-century fortress turned political prison turned museum intrigues me. On the web, the repressions of Prime Minister Salazar's dictatorial rule from 1932 to 1968 are obscure. Through his skillful juggling of competing global interests, he fashioned an image of a nice guy dictator, a competent technocrat who put Portugal's messy economic affairs in order and then, living an austere, simple life, avoided undue participation in the second world war and the apocalyptic trappings of Hitler's Germany.

The Peniche prison tells a different story.

The two-hour bus ride to the seaside town is comfortable, with a delightful view of rolling hills and billboards signaling local cultural trends, and a chance to let my questions for Aida gestate. I choose a guesthouse a short walk from the bus station, the museum, and the beach. I will do a lot of walking during this journey. The guesthouse is a walkup and, with no reception, the neighbors helpfully tell me to call the number on the front door and wait for the fellow who runs the place and its adjacent shop. It's high season for cities and holiday spots in Europe, so I am judicious in researching my lodging sweet spot through the month: under a hundred Euro, well-located, reasonably good reviews, a nice feature or two. But mostly, a comfortable bed, a door that locks, and a functioning bathroom.

The museum, a five-minute walk from the guesthouse, is an impressive physical sight. I enter through reception an hour early, cheerfully greeted by two staff. I get my ticket but choose not to mention my meeting with Aida. I want to wander first.

The Atlantic Ocean laps the rocky shoreline below the building. It's been a while since I've been up close and personal with the Atlantic. The view and the fragrance of sea air are splendid. The fortress was built in 1557-58, with numerous modifications since. Over the centuries, the Portuguese, hemmed in by Spain, looked westward to the sea to find ways to solve their lack of Iberian elbow room. These shores were critical for national defense.

Outside amongst the decayed battlements is an art installation, a tribute to those held here against their will. Inside is a series of exhibitions that tell the story of the human costs of the dictatorship. The methods of ideological propaganda. A ring of dozens of multicolored keys for the cells in which prisoners found themselves, trapped and desperate. Stories of 'anti-fascist unity' cataloguing the history of Portuguese resistance to the regime. Photos of Nazi-style salutes to Salazar. I walk into the former cells and visiting areas. I don't believe in ghosts but touching the bars and walls and prison artifacts gives me an eerie and unsettling feeling, similar to my experience visiting the Khmer Rouge S-21 Prison in Phnom Penh. Here as there: the cruelty was intentional and relentless.

Aida finds me and we go to her office before a walking tour of the exhibits. She projects the warm professionalism of a public museum executive with the razor-sharp perspective of a historian. Taking a seat at her conference table, I ask why Fort Peniche museum was created.

AR: The political prisoners incarcerated here by Salazar's regime demanded that a record of their suffering be left. They asked to preserve the memory of the place. They know that, when they die, the place will speak for them.

The government wanted to build a hotel here, destroying all the prison pavilions, all the memories. That destruction happened in Lisbon with the PIDE (the International State Defense Police), Salazar's political police. Their headquarters, the place where the prisoners were tortured and interrogated, was transformed into luxury flats in the center of Lisbon. The prisoners did not want that to happen here.

BG: *This is the National Museum of Resistance and Freedom. Resistance to what?*

AR: Resistance to Portuguese fascism (*laughs*). It's assumed by the museum that the regime of Salazar was a fascist regime. You can see that at the beginning of the exhibition. At Salazar's working desk at the Palace of Sao Bento, he had a photograph of Mussolini, not his mother or his father. The influence was very clear. And the consequences too. The political prisoners, all of them, called the regime fascist.

BG: *For you, what is fascism?*

AR: How do we characterize it? No freedom of speech, no freedom of thought, no freedom of movement, people cannot go wherever they want. More than three people speaking outside on the street could be arrested for freedom of assembly. What kind of life is that?

And we must speak also about the former colonies. Those people over there, they could not be free. They could not decide their fate or their destiny for their country as they wished. Fascism was this, and it was very violent, very repressive, with a lot of political prisons, scattered all over the empire. It was not only this prison; there were dozens of them. Angola, Mozambique, Guinea-Bissau, Cape Verde, all around the so-called empire. So this was a fascist regime.

BG: *Do you see a connection between colonial empires that brutalized people and exploited them, treating people as subhuman, then, in the 20th century, treating some of their own citizens in the same way?*

AR: It's not an area that I studied. But surely there was the dehumanization of people that think differently, or that speak differently, or that look differently.

BG: *Salazar was a devout Catholic and in authoritarian movements there's often a religious face declaring themselves defenders of traditional values. How important was the support of the church to the Salazar regime?*

AR: The Portuguese Church was run by Cardinal Cerejeira, Salazar's best friend through their whole life. They studied together; they were brought up together. So the Catholic Church was supportive of the regime. On the other hand, there were progressive Catholics that were against the regime, that helped the resistance, that were for the liberation of Angola, Mozambique, and the colonial territories. So it was a two-way thing, that's why some priests were political prisoners too. But of course, the head of the church was with Salazar.

> *How do we characterize it? No freedom of
> speech, no freedom of thought, no freedom of
> movement, people cannot go wherever they want.
> More than three people speaking on the street
> could be arrested. What kind of life is that?*

BG: *Portugal was the last country or empire to give up its colonial empire.*

AR: It was the first to begin in 1415, it was the last to end in 1974.

BG: *How important was control of those colonies to Salazar's propaganda or ideological position?*

AR: Yes, it was, it was. There is this map, you saw it in the exhibition. It's called *Portugal is not a small country*. It overlaps the Portuguese territories on Europe. We have a day of the Portuguese race, June 10. Now it's the day of Portugal. The blacks and the whites, everyone was a Portuguese race. But everyone was not equal as Salazar said. The former colonies were a main feature of the ideology of the empire. Economically, they were fundamental because they allowed Portugal to be economically independent. Salazar had this saying, *'We stand proudly alone'*. In Portuguese, *orgulhosamente sozinhos*. The colonies generated the food, and industries and so on, that kept the regime going.

BG: *Did those economic benefits get down to the common Portuguese?*

AR: No. No. There was one main enterprise, there was CUF (*Companhia União Fabril*) for instance, they had the monopoly on all the ship building. There were a few families, some of them ran the banks, the money. Some the agriculture. Some the industries. And they were all around Salazar. They say Salazar had no money in the bank when he died. I believe that he didn't profit directly.

Because he was like that, a Catholic that lived very strict, very sparse. There were a few families, we know their names. They had to go away from Portugal after the revolution, but then they came back, and all the lands and industries where restituted. We are very peaceful (*laughs*). We did not kill anyone during the revolution.

> *Salazar had this saying, 'We stand proudly alone'. In Portuguese, orgulhosamente sozinhos. The colonies generated the food, and industries that kept the regime going.*

BG: *Describe daily life of the prisoners here.*

AR: The Peniche fortress prison was for prisoners serving long sentences. Before they went to trial, they were in prison in Porto or in the Aljube in Lisbon, also a museum today. When prisoners came here, they knew that they would stay a long time. We have prisoners that spent one or two years, but we have some of them that served 20 years. That's almost a life. They were young men. And then when they get out, they were 50 years old. Life was not easy, some of them were inside the cells 20 or 21 hours per day, alone. This cell (Aida's office is a former prison cell) here was a collective cell for 10-11 prisoners. Some of the prisoners preferred to be alone because the mindset of others could be depressing.

Aida points out that, though her window has a view of the Atlantic, all prison cells had blocked out windows to further torment and isolate the prisoners.

The visits from their families were very controlled by the prison. Families would arrive to Peniche in the 1940s, 50s and 60s with no cars, no roads, it was a very poor country at the time. They would come after six or seven hours by bus with bags of food and clothes, everything they could bring to the prisoners, and the guards would say, no visit. So they would stay here in Peniche with no place to sleep, no money. I would like to stress, the population of Peniche always supported the families of the prisoners and the prisoners themselves by giving them food, by giving them cigarettes, by giving them places to sleep when families were here in the streets alone. So it was not easy to be here, but there was a lot of solidarity. Some of the prisoners learned how to read and write. The prisoners that were educated would teach the others. Of course they could not speak about politics.

BG: *A brutal time.*

AR: It was. The food was very bad. They only had one hour outside in the prison yard if it was not raining. But in Peniche it rains a lot, so they wouldn't go, they would stay inside their own cells. Thinking. One of the prisoners, Domingos Abrantes, 84 years old, I believe, he told me that the prisoners had a lot of time to think. What they were thinking was, first, how to escape. And second, how to resist the oppressor that was inside of the prison, the guards. They would go on strike, they would make many demonstrations like shouting at the windows, asking for better food, or more visiting hours for their families.

BG: *To what degree did Portuguese people know about all of these things through the years?*

AR: It was commonly known what was going on. Here in Peniche everybody knew because they could hear the prisoners, they could see them going inside. I was a child before the revolution. But I knew that people went to prison. There were words and ideas that we could not express. We could not speak badly about Salazar. You could not do that. The communists were our main and most dangerous enemy. I was told that they ate children for breakfast (*laughs*). I remember this. So I think we all knew, no communists around you. But the main thing that the Portuguese didn't like was the colonial war.

It lasted 48 years. Almost half a century. 1926 to 1974.

BG: *How did the regime manufacture consent?*

AR: It is a big question and there are probably a lot of answers. But I believe one of the main reasons is, first, Salazar had all the people with money with him. Because he protected them, so they protected him. And I believe the majority of the people were very ignorant, by political choice. People could not read or write. The illiteracy was huge. Even in 1974 when the revolution came, the majority of people in the country could not read or write.

BG: *You think that was by design?*

AR: It was. It was. It was on purpose, so they could not read or they would not have contact with subversive ideas. So I believe that poverty and ignorance were the main reasons that Salazar could stay in power for so long.

It was commonly known what was going on.

BG: *You said these oligarchs, these conglomerates, these families, for decades, for centuries wanted to hold on to the power and wealth of the country. And therefore having an authoritarian leader where there's no rule of law, where there's no elections, where there's no independent judiciary, where there's no free press, they're able to loot the country.*

AR: Yes. Of course. And they would never be punished. So they could do whatever they wanted. And people were very, very poor.

I'm not saying in Lisbon, because, okay, the services were there, all the banks, all the commerce. But Portugal was a very rural, agricultural country back then. And if you went to Alentejo, the south of Portugal, everyone would work in the fields. They grew wheat. And all the land would belong to one, two, or three men. Families. People were very poor. My grandfather, he was a stonemason, but during the season when they harvested the crops, wheat for example, he would leave his work and go to the fields to get the bread. After a few weeks or months, he would say now we have bread for the whole winter. He could not read and write, my grandfather. So you can see the difference between my grandfather and me. Three generations. And the difference that the revolution could give us. The freedom it could give us. I am a museum director; my grandfather could not read or write.

BG: *Portugal was involved in the slave trade early on, African colonies early on: how did the country embrace that? You have a devout Catholic country. People read the Beatitudes in the Gospels, how you're supposed to treat people. Your museum describes forced labor in the colonies as late as the 1950s, 60s. How does a country that considers itself Christian ideologically defend that?*

AR: Over time, the justifications changed. In the middle ages, like the 15th century, when Portugal began to conquer African places and populations, that was the will of God, because we were Christians. It was the Word of God that we were spreading. Those were savages. They knew no God. We were the Catholics, the good ones that were going to enlighten their way of thinking and their way of life. That's how it began. In human history, slavery has always accompanied us. In ancient Rome, in ancient Greece, Egyptians, all of these ancient civilizations were founded on slave work. Like the Indians in Brazil, like the Native Americans, indigenous people, it was the same: We were the Christians, they were not, they were atheists. We went there and showed them the Word of God. But they had to work for us (*laughs*). Portugal was the first European country in the 19th century to abolish slavery, but I cannot explain to you why the forced labor continued to exist. Why some white landlords in Africa treated the negroes as animals and as slaves. Even in the 20th century that still existed. It's like a contradiction, isn't it? A common feature among several countries, like English and Spanish colonies.

> *Like the Indians in Brazil, like the Native Americans, indigenous people, it was the same: We were showing the Word of God. But they had to work for us.*

BG: *Are there any cautionary tales or lessons learned from Portugal's experience with authoritarianism that you think Americans need to understand?*

AR: I believe they need to understand, not only from the Portuguese example, but the Spanish and the German examples, all of those examples in Europe, Americans are walking on very thin ice. I don't know what may happen if Donald Trump gets into power again. Do American people understand that? I don't know. Biden looks a better man. But the debate was very, very… wow. He could not confront Donald Trump.

I asked Aida for a dinner recommendation and she sent to me to Sardinha. My hotelier suggested the same. Sardinha is on a small cobblestone street with outdoor dining. The waiter seems annoyed that I need only a table for one and that I *não falo português*. But here he is cheerfully laying out several plates of fresh bread, a bean salad, olives, and potato salad. I order the sardines though have a tough time navigating them. The bill comes along with a charge for the four items he graciously provided. "You no eat, you no pay." A first travel crisis. Do I argue? I don't speak his language, I don't know the local dining customs, and I did eat the food. So I pay, then wander back to my room to dose myself for a full night of sleep.

The next morning, I walk to Gamboa Beach (*Praia da Gamboa*) for a formal hello and goodbye to the Atlantic. My journey will conclude in Istanbul's Bosporus Strait, the breadth of the European continent and its varied delights and transport challenges beckoning. My 60 liters of space in the Osprey does not allow for extra shoes. I am wearing a slightly worn Merrill 'lifestyle' pair, black with laces so a restaurant host does not consider me untoward, but with athletic soles for lots of walking and the occasional gym encounter. The map app suggests numerous restaurants but none are open except a garish Burger King across from the beach, the long reach of America's commercial presence.

I have my pastels and espresso in a small neighborhood shop, tiny counter, *nao inglês*, local essentials, before I trek onto the beach. I stare at my phone, jet-lagged, scouting the neighborhood, still looking for a Lisbon hotel, my next stop. Internet travel apps allow a broad opportunity for last minute bookings so the temptation persists to wait for that perfectly priced and placed temporary home. Sometimes you find it. Sometimes you find yourself in a strange city late at night, too tired to read the reviews, stumbling into a regrettable choice.

The beach is great, no one but me wandering the sand. I don't offer prayers for safety, only a monologue to myself on the trip's purpose, with a determination to steal enough fabulous moments to justify the book's title.

And to resolve the questions posed by the project, my own unsupervised, tuition-free field study course.

This being Portugal, I offer a short prayer to Iemanjá, the Brazilian goddess of the sea, for a journey worth sharing.

ROBERT PAXTON
Authoritarian Nationalism

When online lodging choices come in a confusing wave of reviews, locations, features and room prices, a dependable chain can be a safe bet. I reserve an Ibis near the Lisboa Oriente transit station. After a morning walk through the city, I have a call scheduled with the preeminent American expert on fascism, Dr. Robert O. Paxton. Mellon Professor Emeritus of Social Science at Columbia University, specializing in the social and political history of modern Europe, with a Ph.D. from Harvard University, and a Rhodes Scholar M.A. from Oxford University, prolific and often quoted, I feared he might be uninterested in talking to a complete stranger on a subject he had addressed some thousands of times. But he quickly consented and set a call for mid-morning New York time, allowing me to get settled, work on appointments, adjust to jet lag, and do one last review of the highlights I made in his *Anatomy of Fascism.*

C-SPAN founder Brian Lamb once told me of an important interview he scored as a young radio reporter. When he went to replay it, there was… nothing. Since then, I record, when possible, with three devices. Murphy's Law got nothing on me. A Saramonic Bluetooth-enabled dual mic setup feeds to my iPhone, recording on an app with an easy share to my transcriber. My iPad is my backup. And I record in QuickTime on my MacBook Air. On the fly, I use only the Saramonic, which has been a reliable solution. Outside of cables and chargers, and Otter and iCloud accounts, that is my entire technical infrastructure.

Paxton answers the phone in cheerful and friendly form and, after a short exchange of pleasantries, I ask what interested him in writing and teaching about fascism over the years.

BG: *I know you've answered this in print at length, but what is fascism? And has that understanding or sense or relevance of what it is evolved for you in recent years?*

RP: I struggled in my book to come up with a pithy, short definition. And failed. I think it's very hard to encapsulate in a few words, but fascism is a kind of authoritarian nationalism, that is distinct from the old conservative forms like dictatorship, in that it wants mass support, it wants an enthusiastic crowd. And so that's what was new about it. We'd had all sorts of forms of dictatorship and conservative authoritarianism who wanted to keep the crowd silent. But fascism wanted to generate enthusiasm. And I think that's the core of it, it's authoritarian nationalism, with an enthusiastic mass base.

BG: *In a compendium of articles about fascism, you wrote a piece indicating you've changed your mind and now believe Donald Trump is a fascist.*

RP: Trump is hard to pin down because the only thing that seems to motivate him is greed for money and surrounding himself with personal admiration. And so it's a very private, kind of personal set of attributes. But the force of it politically is very close to fascism. I didn't want to call him a fascist for a while. The differences is the classical fascists, particularly Mussolini and Hitler, subjected businessmen to national needs. And they had four-year plans or five-year plans and rearmament projects that were not the first choice of capitalists though they were delighted to have it when socialism frightened them enough. Now in Trump's case it's just pure personal satisfaction. It's a very individual thing for him to get the adulation of crowds and to be able to collect rent money while he's President. Dismissing scornfully the tradition of putting his assets into a blind trust while he's President. It's that personalized, self-aggrandizement. It's hard to fit into any kind of political category, it's just plain old greed and thirst for adulation.

> *I think it's very hard to encapsulate in a few words, but fascism is a kind of authoritarian nationalism, with an enthusiastic mass base.*

BG: *When you published* Anatomy of Fascism, *the* Washington Post *praised you for thoughtfully mapping out the descent of a civilized people, first the Italians, then the Germans, into a primal state, a state of being ruled by mythology, symbol, and emotion. How do you think the American people, the supposed beacons of liberal democracy and higher education, science, and technology, descended into a primal state ruled by mythology, symbol and motion in this adoration of Donald Trump?*

RP: First of all, they didn't all do that when Trump was elected president. He was chosen by the Electoral College, which is a very old and inaccurate reflection, an 18th-century device to keep the ordinary people from expressing their will too clearly. And he did not win the popular vote. So you're talking about 40 percent of Americans, maybe 45 or even 49 percent of Americans. But there are a great many other people who are sort of horrified by him. But it's difficult for them to mobilize their opposition because of the Electoral College. I think we desperately, most urgently need a constitutional amendment providing for the direct election of the president. We're the only wealthy, powerful country in the world that has this 18th-century indirect election of president, it's grotesque. So Trump never had the support of everybody. Indeed he never had a popular majority.

BG: *Do you think there's always been a fascist or authoritarian underbelly to American political culture?*

RP: Yeah, I do. I think that every country does, in different ways because each national instance is unique. But the United States has always had those elements. In the South, there was the existence of slavery and all the mental contortions that went into justifying or even praising it. So there's a big chunk of the country right there. I mean, it was the Alien and Sedition Acts right back in the beginning of our country. When the country is under pressure and under threat, there are people who think that you have to crack down on dissent. So those viruses or drivers are there right from the beginning and affect some regions more than others.

BG: *You describe in* Anatomy of Fascism *the extreme conditions that motivated Italians and Germans to embrace fascism, the economic and political phenomena from World War One. What are the corollary events now, justified or not, that are driving this kind of fresh appetite of Trump supporters for the things that he's advocating?*

RP: I don't see them, objectively; we have close to full employment, the stock market is bubbling away upwards. But there's the realm of perception. There's this baffling phenomenon, life is relatively good for Americans, we haven't been defeated in a war like Germany, we haven't been undergoing a Great Depression, like the world in 1929. Objectively, things look pretty good and yet everybody's mood is sour. There's a lot of journalistic comment about that, and no one quite knows what to make of it. I find it frankly baffling; the objective conditions would not seem to sponsor that kind of desperate craving for some kind of authority.

> *The United States has always had those elements. In the South, there was the existence of slavery, and all the mental contortions that went into justifying or even praising it.*

BG: *One of the problems with thinking about fascism is that we've seen all the Holocaust movies and we've seen Il Duce speaking to throngs from a Roman balcony and we think that's fascism, and we look around* *and we don't see quite the same thing here. What do you think would be a 2025 American version of fascism?*

RP: I think that Trump's rallies are a very powerful visual representation. And they're not so different from the Italian and German mass rallies of Hitler and Mussolini. There's absorption of the individuals into an excited mass. It must be a very exhilarating thing, if you're not repelled by it, to be in that crowd and swept up by the excitement. It must be a very visceral kind of frenzy. And those rallies are his stock in trade. And I guess that would be the visual symbol of his electoral power.

BG: *Is it simply his need for gratification? Or do you think there is a strategy, mapping the way that the rallies are affecting public opinion?*

RP: I've been assuming that it's his show. And I think that there's a kind of feedback loop, it works, he gets all sorts of gratification out of the response of the crowd, so he goes out and does it again.

> *I think that Trump's rallies are a very powerful visual representation. And they're not so different from the Italian and German mass rallies of Hitler and Mussolini. There's absorption of the individuals into an excited mass.*

BG: *A few days ago the Supreme Court ruled that presidents in certain circumstances have immunity from criminal prosecution. Does that concern you? And where does something like that end up if Trump is reelected?*

RP: I think it's extremely dangerous if he's president. Last time he was a rather lazy president, went out and played golf. And he promised to do a lot of things that he never quite got around to and that might happen again. But this time he sounds a little more serious. I think it's a very, very bad decision and is going to do a lot of harm.

BG: *What do you think good patriotic Americans should be doing now to avoid a fascist future?*

RP: The first thing to do is to elect a Democrat in November. The most important thing for Americans to do is to vote and vote against Trump. If he's not elected, he'll say it's a phony election. The poll workers who are both Democrats and Republicans keep defending what they do. I think the electoral process is fairly clean in this country. He hasn't won any law cases about the last election. I think what he would do when elected, he could this time be a little more assiduous.

BG: *There was one passage in* Anatomy of Fascism *where you write, 'deeper preconditions of fascism lay in the late 19th century revolt against the dominant liberal faith in individual liberty, reason, natural human harmony, and progress'. That was well before 1914. Do you see something similar happening now, that civil institutions taken for granted are now boring to people, that people are revolting against them and want something different?*

RP: Maybe so. There's one body of thought that makes race an important motivator here. There has been, in fact, some important progress made in race relations in the United States. There are black people now in all professions, in all walks of life, and many of them are doing well. And it's aroused a backlash. There are people who believe that white males are being discriminated against. I think you can have a lot of trouble proving that in any empirical way. But the sense is that the former way with which white males eased into leadership positions has been altered, it's not quite as automatic as it was. I think that's emotionally upsetting to a lot of people. People who are turned down for law school or don't get a job and see a black or brown person getting those positions. And so there is I think an emotional groundswell that runs counter to the general feeling a generation ago that these things were going to happen. And that these things were progressive, and we should support them. And now there are people who claim that they're paying the price and are not getting ahead and not getting the job or not getting into law school because of affirmative action. I think there is a kind of mood shift there.

> *The first thing to do is to elect a Democrat in November. The most important thing for Americans to do is to vote and vote against Trump. If he's not elected, he'll say it's a phony election.*

And there's another rhythm, which is the American position after World War Two. For temporary and factitious reasons, we were number one, and it wasn't because we were better, it was because everybody else had been knocked out. And now everybody else has come back. And we're finding the global environment more competitive than it used to be. But I do think that there is a lot of insecurity out there among people who feel threatened. I thought of it as a race thing first, but it's obviously a gender thing also. And I think that maybe explains this strange misfit between objective prosperity and this subjective fear and discontent that we are seeing.

BG: *Any final thoughts about where the country might be going?*

RP: The next election is perhaps the most important one in American history. I think it's a real fork in the road. And even if a Democrat is elected president, it doesn't mean we're out in the clear because these people, the other side, is going to say it's fake and there could well be violence after it.

RUI CARVALHEIRA
Lusotropicalism and the Sermon of the Fishes

After a morning walk through the city, I meet Rui Carvalheira in front of the Jeronimos Monastery, jammed on this sunny Saturday with tourist buses. It's a grand site in Manueline, a late Gothic architectural style, erected in the early 16th century in Belem parish where Vasco de Gama launched his first journey to discover a sea route to India, enabling Portugal's eventual colonial empire from Africa to Asia.

Rui Carvalheira is Lisbon-born, has written, edited, and directed several documentaries and television programs, and he has published three books on Portuguese history, including *The Two Faces of Salazar* on 'the ambiguity of Portugal's most controversial figure of the 20th century'. It's the world expo, not the monastery, that most interests Rui for the purposes of our conversation. We wander through the aging monuments before walking through the park and settling into an outdoor bistro.

RC: In Belem in 1940, during the Second World War, the Portuguese dictatorship presented the Portuguese World Exposition. They pretended to show the colonies, the empire, and the Portuguese to the world. Even if all of Europe was at war, here we lived in peace thanks to Salazar. The monastery is also important, built by King Manuel I in 1501 to celebrate de Gama's journey to India. It took about a century to be built. And the garden we are walking in was built for the exposition. Those big monuments celebrate the Portuguese discovery. You can see the coats of arms from different parts of the empire. This is an important place to understand the Portuguese identity and the Portuguese dictatorship. It was very connected to the idea of empire. Everybody was losing their empires. In the end, it was the war in the colonies that made the government fall. It was the revolt of the soldiers; they made the coup d'état.

BG: *And the motivation for the explorations with de Gama? Commercial? Military? Political?*

RC: And religious. This was a little bit of everything. First, we were kind of stonewalled against Spain and the sea. We had no possibilities to expand inland. So we did the expansion overseas. In those times, the commerce that came from the east was controlled mainly by the Italian city states in the Mediterranean. They started to study the idea that if we could circumnavigate Africa, we could get to India, and we could build a new commercial line. So it was the big project of the Portuguese monarchy, how to get to India and how to exploit those resources and the African resources. Our colonial empire was different from the British, the French and the Spanish because we did not possess big chunks of land, we controlled ports and important commercial cities. We controlled the commerce. We had a small army and we had few people so we could not conquer India. So we controlled some places, important city states and sites and that was our empire. It was mainly commercial, but it was also a political statement. Spain was a much bigger country, so it was a kind of statement to the Spanish to say, look, we are small, but we are not weak.

BG: *Explain the religious motivation.*

RC: One of the ideas that supported the expansion was, we're gonna take the truth, religion, to the pagans. So we went to Africa to teach them about Christ and convert them to Catholicism, the same in India. This was because, in those times, in the 14th, 15th century, religion was a main player in politics in Europe. There were religious wars. And it was a kind of a way to support legitimacy. The king was appointed by God. And so if the king wanted to be legitimate, he had to support the church and the church, in contrast, would support him. The church in Portugal was very, very, very important to the dictatorship, it played a big part in the Salazar system, but was also a big player in this 16th century system.

BG: *How much of this was a cynical estimation, that we needed to motivate people to risk their lives on colonial voyages and wars, but we also needed to assuage our own guilt at the brutality with which we're creating colonies?*

RC: I think you can't really separate the two. In my personal opinion, it was used as justification. That was God will? No, that was *your* will. It was not really a religious thing. I believe that some people really believed that it was God's will. But the political elites used it as a way to control the population and to legitimatize their interests.

BG: *Today as well, people who have an ideological position wrap it in…*

RC: You look to the Middle East, it's the same today. We have always been a relatively poor country. The population has low literacy, traditionally. When you have a very poor and very ignorant population, religion is very important to communicate and to control the people. Because people don't know how to read, so they build those beautiful pieces in the churches, the paintings, to show the faithful the message because you can't read it.

It was a way to say, we're God's chosen people, otherwise we would not have been able to build this. In Portugal, Catholicism was always the only religion. Protestants never had a real presence here. And we have the Muslim heritage, because we were once occupied by the Muslim empire from North Africa.

> *The population has low literacy traditionally. When you have a very poor and very ignorant population, religion is very important to communicate and to control the people.*

BG: *In Spanish colonies in Latin America, there were a few famous priests who saw the brutality and questioned it, then came back and, at great personal risk, presented what was happening to the royalty. Did that happen in Portugal as well?*

RC: Yes, Jesuit priest Saint António Vieira saw the same things. He wrote a famous sermon. It was the sermon to the fishes. It was irony, if the men don't listen to me, I will pray to the fishes. And in the sermon, he talked about the injustice that was being made meted out against the natives from Brazil, this was not God's will. But the higher up positions in the church, they always went along with the regime, except during the First Republic. With the kings, even in the fights against Spain, the church was always flickering from one place to the other, because in some times during the 14th century, there were two popes, one in France, one in Italy. And it's symptomatic of the use of religion for politics and the Portuguese were alternating between supporting the pope from Avignon or the pope from Rome. I believe that some people really believed, yes, no question. But in terms of politics, I think it was mainly useless. Because Portugal was a major player, it was an important part of the legitimacy of power.

BG: *The genocide of Native Americans—and slavery—was represented as God's will. The United States of America as a divine project.*

RC: American exceptionalism. It's not a new thing in history, we in Portugal have always claimed some kind of exceptionalism, our empire was justified by the new state, by Salazar, as a Portuguese. A different kind of colonialism. We did not have slaves, we did not mistreat the natives, a way of justifying to everybody outside, no, no, we were not bad colonists, we were the good colonists.

BG: *I was married to a Brazilian woman for some years. And she claimed that the Spanish did not take on Latin American wives and* *create families together, but that the Portuguese created families with indigenous Brazilians. She presented the idea in more colorful language. Any truth to that?*

RC: Yeah, it's not totally wrong for a few things. First. We were few. So when we arrived to the places to occupy them, we had to mingle with the population. Because there were not enough Portuguese. See, we are 10 million today. When we got to Brazil, we were about two, maybe three million people. Impossible to colonize a country that big. So we had to mingle with the population. But there was also another thing, an idea that came from the dictatorship. *Lusotropicalism.* It was the idea that Portugal was different because Portuguese mingled with the population wherever they went and created a unique society. This was propaganda. In fact, Portuguese did mingle with some Brazilians, but they did it because they didn't have enough people to colonize and occupy the country. And those people with whom they mingled, were always inferior. Okay, we created a new class society in Brazil, with the whites at the top. And then the darker you were, the lower down you found yourself. That was an idea that Salazar exploited all over the world during the 20th century, to justify why we would not leave our colonies. But it really was, well, it was political bullshit. We went there to enslave the natives. The Indians were not used to the work so they kept dying. That's why we began to bring Africans to Brazil, because the ones there were not good workers. But we went to Brazil to exploit Brazil, it was not developed, the people lived in nature, with nature, and so for us Portuguese in 1498, when we got there, we looked at that and said, 'Oh, there's nobody here'. It was full of people!

BG: *Was there resistance?*

RC: In Brazil, in the beginning, there was not much resistance because they'd never seen people like us. The guy that sent a chronicle back to the king said they received us with open hearts. They had never seen white people, so they believed that we were gods, we came from the sea. Only after that, the real occupation began. But we were not as violent as the Spanish.

You have to get back to the First Republic. In 1910, the Portuguese defeated the monarchy, and installed a republic. It took 16 years and then it fell. During those 16 years, it was a chaotic situation. You had governments that lasted for one day, and there were bombs exploding in the streets. Leaders were always fighting with each other. So the people, the middle class, the bourgeoisie, were fed up. And then in 1926, the military defeated the First Republic with a coup. Salazar did not participate because he was a university teacher, he was not military. And during the first two years, the New Republic, it was a big confusion among the military because the only plan they had was to overthrow the government. What to do next? No idea.

BG: *They were against the republic.*

RC: Yes, because they wanted peace. And the church is very important because with the First Republic, expropriation of the church ended the church. The First Republic was a romantic idea, now we're going to teach everybody in the country, ignorance will be gone. And the main focus of ignorance was the church. But the fact is, it was only applied to maybe five to 10 percent of the population. The rest of the population was very poor, very ignorant. And so they were under control of the church, which was a big part of their lives. So when you got a new regime with people that said, no more religion, people didn't buy it. The military that made the coup were conservative. And they were intelligent enough to understand that religion was a big part of things.

Salazar is celebrated for two things. Portugal was always losing money. And when he came to power as finance minister, he did manage to get the budget right. And then he brought peace to the streets. These two things were the motive for celebration and pride in the beginning.

> *You had governments that lasted for one day,*
> *and there were bombs exploding in the streets.*
> *Leaders were always fighting with each other.*
>
> *So the people, the middle class,*
> *the bourgeoisie, were fed up.*

BG: *Was there a sentiment that, okay, Salazar, you're doing fine, but at some point, we want elections? Or were people with a history of monarchy not that interested?*

RC: Yes. There was, but mainly in the elites. The politics was something from and for the aristocracy, the elites, and the people did not matter. So there were some people, mainly the Democrats that come from the First Republic. But most people, didn't know what democracy was, they had never lived in a democracy. For them, they just wanted bread and peace and be well. So the revolt was always very small, very concentrated in the echelons of power. So yes, there was a movement. But Salazar was, in his own words, anti-liberal, anti-parliamentarism, anti-democratic. He didn't want a parliament.

BG: *Not that he needed justification if he had the military and the church, but his justification was it's a nice idea, democracy, but we need to achieve these things. And to do that…*

RC: We needed order and peace. And then Salazar was also a nationalist, he believed in empire. The empire was the only place where Portugal had riches, the mainland was poor. When it came to Angola, some of the resources really never trickled down to the people. Some people went to Angola lived way better than in Portugal, but it was a small minority. The thing was when Salazar came to power, authoritarian dictatorships were seen as…

BG: *…normal.*

RC: Valid government systems. Because we didn't have the Second World War yet. People hadn't yet seen what authoritarians could do. And he did bring some peace and some order. And the country began to work a little bit better. So in the beginning, he was celebrated, even in England, our oldest ally. Finally Portugal had a ruler who could govern.

BG: *There was a long-standing financial relationship between the British and Portugal.*

RC: The British always had an alliance with Portugal, because it was a way to stop the Spanish to control the peninsula. It was not that they really liked us. We were used. It was useful for both, we needed them to stop the Spanish because otherwise we could not defeat their military. They needed us to be here to avoid the Spanish having control of the entire peninsula. And then you have to understand that Salazar was clearly the best prepared politician of them all. He came to power as simply the finance minister. He had no leverage whatsoever over the military. He was the only one who had a real political project. He was maybe the only one who did what he wanted to do. And that made it possible for him to grow inside the government. And then he made the decision, it was a famous decision, that was what eventually led him to control the entire government. He said okay, now, I agree to be finance minister. Okay, just to understand, he was a famous teacher, so everybody recognized him as a master of public finances. And he said, okay, I go to the government, but no minister can claim any expenses without my approval. With this small play, he controlled the entire government. And then the new state, *Estado Novo*, the dictatorship only began in 1933. Basically he joined with two people and wrote the constitution that came to be the new state and that constitution was authoritarian. The parliament existed; it was just there to support the decisions of the government.

BG: *Were there elections?*

RC: In theory, according to the constitution, it was the president who chose the prime minister. So the elections were for the president. Presidents came from the military through the entire dictatorship. And he made some kind of agreement with the military that was, okay, I give you the money to modernize your armed forces and to do whatever you want. And in exchange, you don't mess in politics. And they agreed because they were not really prepared for government. And this new constitution was mainly it, you had a parliament, but the parliament did not have legislative capacity. It was just there to support the decisions Salazar made. And the elections were not universal voting. You had to have enough money to vote, you had to know how to read and to write. So it was a way of excluding 80 or 90 percent of the population. And they always won during the entire 46 years of dictatorship. The only party, there were no political parties allowed. The party from the government always went with 98, 99, 100 percent. They always kept all the parliamentary seats, always for them. So, really the only power was the government and the government was controlled by Salazar. Technically he could be dismissed by the president. But he never was.

BG: *When did dissent become serious?*

RC: In the 1930s, in the beginnings, some people, the more literate, began to understand what was going on. So there was a protest movement. But Salazar used one thing, the fear of the communists. And so they labeled everyone in the opposition as communists, so we had to exterminate communism. And you know, you have to understand that when you arrest and beat enough people, the rest will comply. They might not like it, but they will comply. It was not like the civil war in Spain, there were no mass shootings. But there were people killed, there were people arrested. And the biggest thing of the dictatorship for me was the economic censorship. He built a system in which was not possible to climb, there was no social ladder. It's like, for him the social life, the ideal social society was from the Middle Ages. Everybody knew their place. Nobody messed around. Because, he liked to say, that social mobility tended to chaos, everybody stayed in the places where they were born and nobody climbed up or down.

BG: *And maybe that was God's will?*

RC: And maybe that was God's will. The Church supported him from the beginning because he was a very religious man.

BG: *And the church benefited financially and otherwise from…*

RC: He gave back everything that the Republic had taken from them. They paid no taxes and they were listened to by the government. He was a very intelligent man, you have to understand. He had a political sense. He understood the country and he understood the moment, and he used that. In the 30s, you had revolts. You had some militaries that revolted, you had the union workers revolting, you had some left-wing revolts, but they all failed. And it was during the first 10 years, as he was consolidating his power, he was pushing aside every opposition. Even on the right, there was a faction that was much more radical than him. He managed to wipe out the opposition on the right and on the left. And in the 1940s, there was nobody but him. It took him 10 years. And from then, he was in the media, in the schools, in the workplace, he built Portugal as a corporate state. Everything was controlled by the government, even the holidays. He built an institution for the holidays for the people. So you couldn't do your holidays. You had to go on holidays that the unions create, so there was no liberty whatsoever to do anything you wanted.

If you stayed away from politics, you could live your life. No problem. The thing was, you would never get rich. You would never get up the social ladder. If you complied then everything was fine, nobody was going to hurt you. If you tried to complain, you probably ended up in prison. The police, the secret police were very, very, present. It was very hard. There were people tortured and all those things. There was a censorship. You couldn't print a newspaper without passing it by them, they chose what could and could not be said. You couldn't choose a job, you had to be in a corporation to apply for a job. And the corporation was controlled by the state. So everything was controlled by the state.

> *You had to have enough money to vote, you had to know how to read and write. It was a way of excluding 80 or 90 percent of the population.*
>
> *And they always won during the entire 46 years of dictatorship.*

BG: *At the Peniche Museum, I was struck by the fact that both the director and the exhibits did not hesitate to say that Salazar was fascist. As you know, outside of Portugal, and maybe inside as well, there's this perception that, well, he wasn't fascist, it was kind of fascism lite. And he did some good things. And he was not like Hitler or Mussolini.*

RC: First, I don't know if he was a fascist or just authoritarian in terms of life in the country. The true fascism was Italian. You have some similarities, like everything is controlled by the state. The unions, the jobs, the economy, everything is controlled by the state, there's no capitalism, there's no communism, in that sense, it's similar to the Italians. The Germans, they built a mass movement, they brought the people to the street. In Portugal, there was never a mass movement.

BG: *Was that because it was not a culturally Portuguese thing to do?*

RC: No. Salazar was terrified of the idea that the population would come onto the streets. So all the efforts were made from the beginning to keep the population away from politics. And the only mass movement you had was *Mocidade Portuguesa*, the Portuguese youth movement. That was like the brown shirts, but without beating people in the streets.

It was different from the Spanish because it didn't come from a civil war. The Spanish had a very specific type of fascism because it came from a terrible civil war where hundreds of thousands of people died. Salazar played both sides during the Second World War. He sold tungsten ore to the English and the Germans, almost until the end of the war.

BG: *There's the famous scene in the movie* Casablanca *where they were selling transit visas to Lisbon.*

RC: Yeah. Because from Lisbon, you got to the United States and he did play both sides. Like any politician, his main preoccupation from the beginning was keeping power. Salazar cultivated an idea that he was not the politician, in the way that politics was a nasty, ugly, dirty thing. No, he was not a politician, but he was the best politician of them all. And all he did was always from the beginning, in the interest of keeping himself in power. Because he never married. He had a voice like this (*mimics high pitched voice*), he was not good for massive demonstrations.

BG: *Paint me a positive portrait of Salazar, what can be said good about him.*

RC: He was not a violent man, he saw violence as a means to an end, not an end in itself. And he did keep the country quiet and peaceful. And he did regenerate the public finances. And, in fact, he stopped the real hard right that exists in Portugal. Because there was a faction in the far right that was much more radical than Salazar. And he did stop them. But besides that, I cannot say good things about him.

BG: *What were his motivations? Service, holding power?*

RC: It's very difficult to answer that. I believe that there was some sense of public service in him. He saw the world with very medieval eyes. Like the church was here, the king was here. And he was the king, the church and the king were here and nobody moved up and down and everybody was quiet. And everybody knew their places. And there was no chaos, no instability. Stability was the main thing. I think that once he started climbing the ladder, maybe he got a little bit fascinated by his own power. I think so. The first time he came to Lisbon, he was teaching in Coimbra. It was all in the first few years of the Republic. He was invited to be the finance minister in 1926, and he came, and he saw things and he went, he didn't accept. And the thing he said, 'I didn't accept because I didn't believe in parliament.' But the thing is, he had a very, very political keen eye. And he saw that the guy that was inviting him would not last long. So it's very difficult for me say that it was only public service. Because there were some movements from the beginning that you could see, this guy was a real politician. And he was seeing things that others didn't. And he was moving accordingly to it. He did it. He (and his successor) spent 48 years in power.

He saw the world in medieval eyes.
The church was here, the king was here.
Nobody moved up and down and everybody
was quiet. And everybody knew their places.
And there was no chaos, no instability.

BG: *After World War Two, when did legitimate opposition movements, democratic movements begin to develop?*

RC: They were never allowed. In 1945, at the end of the war, Salazar made a very famous public speech, he said the next elections would be as free as in the free England. And so everybody believed that, okay, now Europe was coming and progress was coming and we were going to be a democracy. But he didn't. It was a statement to pacify the English and other allies. At the end of the second world war, Portugal and Spain were the only authoritarian regimes left in Europe. And so they needed to find a way to stay without being overpowered by the allies that had won the war. So he made this promise to appease the English and make people believe that, yes, the election…

BG: *You can't keep that up for 20 years.*

RC: Because the elections never were free, because the parties weren't allowed to participate in elections. Ballot boxes were always delivered to the places where the votes were already full. There were more votes for the government than there were people. So, a farce.

BG: *So it took two, three decades for elections…*

RC: 1945 to 1974. Almost 30 years. After World War Two, you had some people that were very, very important. Mário Soares most of all. Soares went on to become the President of the Republic of

Portugal. He's probably the most important politician of our democracy. And he was a known opponent to the state from the beginning. He was arrested, he was deported to São Tomé and Príncipe. In those times after the second World War, people were forming opposition movements, but it was always clandestine. They were arrested, beaten. The Communist Party was always in opposition.

BG: *So after World War Two, you had a lot of European countries giving up their colonies, you had more mass media availability through radio, then television, you had a growth of liberal democracy throughout, certainly, Western Europe. At what point did the Portuguese people, you mentioned the bourgeoisie, or a significant part of the population say, we we've waited long enough. Especially because Salazar stayed in power until he had a stroke. So it wasn't as though he said, okay, I am ready to leave the scene.*

RC: No, he never thought it was time to leave the scene. The Portuguese did believe that democracy was coming after World War Two, because of those proclamations of free elections, but people were arrested. In the supposed free elections, people were prohibited from voting. In the end, he won the election. And he said to the world, 'See, the Portuguese want me. I made the election and I won again'. Of course, elections were not free. Of course, people weren't allowed to vote, people were arrested before the evening, before the day.

Now, we live in neoliberal times, we people think that we are important enough to change things, we can do anything. I think the Portuguese in those times, they felt similar, that they wanted things to change, but they didn't know how to do it. And they never saw it coming, because they never believed it was possible because they had always lived under the regime. It was coming from 1926. So in 1945, we had had 20 years of regime. People had no tools to make the transformation. And the police, the secret police in those days after the war, they were very active, arresting people. Mário Soares and others came from the elites. So they had access to foreign countries and foreign press, and they knew what was happening. But in Portugal, the common citizen, had no BBC to see or to watch or to listen. They only had the Portuguese mass media, which was completely under the control of the state. So people believed that it was like a dream. It never really worked, democracy in Portugal, even in the First Republic, so the common citizen, they didn't know what democracy is.

No, he never thought it was time to leave the scene.

BG: *Are there a significant number of Portuguese today, especially the older generation, who miss Salazar, who say we need another Salazar?*

RC: I think today the world is very confusing. Frightening. And people I think miss the simple times. And what you say, it's right. It's mostly the old generation. But not only, the new Portuguese right wing party has some youngsters voting in mass. I think it's like a sense of nostalgia. Get into simple times. Every time things get complicated, and get busy and chaotic, people miss the simple times. I think in part it's that. And I believe that some part of the population is truly nationalist. They miss the grandness of the Republic, of the Portuguese empire. And some people voted for these parties as a way of protesting against the system. In the elections for the legislature, the Portuguese right-wing party had almost 20 percent. But in the following election in June, the European one, they only got nine. Half of the population that votes is protesting against the system.

BG: *Are there things about Trump's posture and behavior that are familiar to you from your understanding of the Salazar years?*

RC: Yes, neo-liberalism created a sense of false meritocracy. The idea that you have what you deserve. Here that creates a sense of humiliation for the people, for the poor people or the lower class. We work 10 hours a day and we can't even buy a house. And now these guys come in telling us, that's because we don't deserve it. Because we don't work enough. So this false meritocracy, this idea humiliated people and some people are voting in these populist demagogues that say, okay, now we're going to put the women back in the home and we're going to expel all the foreigners, that will fix it, and we're going to put police in the streets and end the violence. But people don't have any idea what they're going to do to change the situation.

It's Iike Trump when he says no, no, it's the Mexicans that come here destroying social security and we're going to build a wall and they will not come, it is bullshit. That isn't the problem and never will be. People no longer trust the elites, and this is a thing that happened in Europe. The left-center made a huge mistake in the 90s when they validated neo-liberalism, and they said, okay, we are no longer fighting for equal distribution, we are fighting for getting equal opportunities. And it's not really a solution because if your father is rich and mine is poor, you will have much more opportunities. But this came attached to the idea that if there are equal opportunities, what you get is what you deserve. And people see and know that there are no equal opportunities. And so you cannot tell me that I have what I deserve, because I didn't have the same opportunities that you had. And so when people say you have what you deserve, you are humiliating me, and the left wing in Europe, those guys like Blair, even Merkel in Germany, they validated the idea that liberals in the market will solve problems of distribution and inequalities. And all we as government have to do is to make sure that people have the same opportunities. This is a fallacy. But it gets in the center of the political system. And so the proletarian people, they look and see that—okay, proletarian is like a concept because we didn't really have an industrial revolution in Portugal—no one in politics is representing us. Everyone in politics is representing big economic interests. And so we're going to revolt, and what we do in a revolt, you vote in the guy that is against that, because he wants to get his hands on the power. So he has enough intelligence to see, okay, if I say that, people will vote for me because I will finish all this corruption. That's one of the things that made the right wing grow.

Another thing is, and that's also, in my opinion, a left-wing mistake—and I always voted for the left—but I recognize the mistake, once they disassociate themselves from the working-class, from the fight for better prosperity, better distribution, fair opportunities, that equality, they tend to get attached to the minority things like the general politics that went up and created the woke culture. Most people don't see the relevance. So they began to dissociate from the left. In Portugal, we always were a little bit of a traditional conservative country. Those movements are seen by the people as wanting to end the family, which is completely wrong, and it's hyperbole, but the left in Europe are now closed in a loop that they built themselves. They represent the minorities, which are very important things, but they are not determinant to...

BG: *By minorities you mean what?*

RC: Like gay rights. The immigrants that came to Portugal needed to work. But one thing that you might think, okay, we need the immigrants so let's build a system to import them and to assimilate them into society. But I think it's the thing for the Portuguese left, it's the left, the far left, it's like all the immigrants are good. All the white males are bad because they are imperialists. So, this kind of simplification built the left system, and most people don't see the relevance. Which is in my opinion, a big mistake, because the thing that always marks left politics is the fight against inequality, the fight against the big differences in property and wealth, and those things, they're more important now than ever, but no one is defending them. So the people on the right are saying, I'm going to close the borders and we will expel all the Asians and Africans and everything is going to be okay. Which is nonsense because we need those people to work. But when things get complicated, people tend to look for easy solutions, as if the Mexicans are the problem. If we expel all the Mexicans, all will be good. It's not the problem. The problem is the political and economic system, but that is much more difficult to change.

I walk to a now favorite outdoor spot, with an expansive view. The waitress, likely the owner, as she bounces around directing her small crew, shows her disdain for my choice of Mateus. I explain it was the favorite of my teenage friends and I wondered how it would taste 50 years on in its country of origin. She insists on bringing me samples of Portuguese white wines, explaining the geography and history of the varietals. I select one.

The next day, after a leisurely walk around town with an old friend from the States, I check out of the Ibis and head over to the Lisboa Oriente station for the midnight bus ride. I expect to take trains the rest of the way but a bus experience seems adventurous and nostalgic. I get there early and, in the maze of signs and numbers, it is not entirely clear where I board. I walk around with bags in tow, up and down escalators, until I am sure I have it right. *Bus company. Boarding slot. Bus number.* People are dutifully resting in an early queue. There is a light odor of sweat, urine, and fast food. With an hour to spare, I head over to the adjacent Vasco de Gama shopping mall. The Portuguese frequently honor their iconic explorer who opened the spice routes to India. In addition to procuring pepper and cinnamon, de Gama looted ports, cut off the hands and noses of offending adversaries, shot cannon balls into cities that did not provide a suitably warm welcome, enslaved natives, and looted then burned alive a ship of

400 Muslim pilgrims travelling from Calicut to Mecca. Twenty children of desperate mothers were given safety on the condition they be converted to Christianity.

I need a place in the vast mall to pick up toiletries and some healthy snacks and spot my favorite Brazilian retailer, Boticário. I wander in to kill some time. After a purchase, I change clothes in the mall men's room, then sit on a bench watching the shoppers go by as departure time approaches. A female janitor stops in front of me and scolds me in Portuguese, pointing to the iPhone I have placed at my side. "Don't leave there, too dangerous," she instructs in Portuguese. Yes, momma, I promise. The kindness of strangers.

Then it's time to board. Several people approach me, asking for money. I decline. As we board, I down a sleeping pill and get ready to test the ALSA website's promise of a long comfortable overnight ride to Madrid.

CHAPTER 2

SPAIN

Franco Kills the Republic

Whereupon the author arrives from the overnight bus ride from hell… a visit to Picasso's Guernica *at Madrid's Reina Sofía museum… Journalist Carlos Sardiña Galache explains the state of Spanish politics… a chat with* Spain in our Hearts *and* King Leopold's Ghost *author Adam Hochschild… a walking tour of the Spanish Civil War and a Bacalao a la Catalana lunch with author and Barcelona guide Nick Lloyd.*

I chose the ALSA overnight bus because the train route from Lisbon to Madrid requires too long a detour. The company promised a comfortable, restful trip with reclining seats, allowing for a solid, deep sleep. They lied. The trip starts with passengers watching videos and making calls as I realize that seats allow only a precious few inches of recline. Then stretches of bumpy road, then a grudging acceptance that I will simply will not sleep, then, finally, a few hours rest. We arrive in the sparse Madrid station and, with a spurt of adrenaline, I decide to take the Metro to the hotel. It is unreasonably ambitious to expect an 8am check in but the receptionist cheerfully hands me my key and, ecstatic, I set up camp in bed for the morning.

After five hours of alternatively dozing and reviewing notes, I make my way out to the Plaza del Callao for a tapas lunch.

Museo Nacional Centro de Arte Reina Sofia, Madrid

This is my second viewing of Pablo Picasso's *Guernica*, my first a half century ago as a young boy.

I grew up in a Brooklyn neighborhood called East New York, near my birthplace of Brownsville. Mike Tyson often brags how he and his Bedford-Stuyvesant friends used to come into ENY to steal bikes. Three kids once tried, but my bike was new, and though one of the kids jabbed me with a knife, I refused to get off. I suppose I was 10 or 11. They warned me not to call an adult nearby, but I am bad at taking direction and stubborn, and they fled after I called out for help.

I lived in the Linden Houses, a post-WWII government housing project. Lindens are large trees with pale green leaves, often planted in urban areas. The central grassy areas between 64-unit buildings were surrounded by chains, with prohibitions against playing on the sparse greenery. Stickball—and every other ball sport—was also forbidden. Running from NYC housing police was the principal athletic activity.

I once figured that my block had more people living on it than my ex-wife Jane's Iowa town. It was a great childhood. Jews, Italians, African Americans, Puerto Ricans, 50 nationalities all battling their way into better circumstances. If my mom was not home and I hurt myself, I could go to Bernice (Bunny) Schwartz or any of a dozen other women in the building and I would be just fine.

My dad Sol drove a taxi. Sometimes he took me along and, because I was terribly cute as I talked up passengers, I earned tips. In our ethnically diverse Linden projects, the importance of education was an article of faith. The entrance to our apartment, both my parents were high school dropouts during the Depression, sported a bookcase with the World Book encyclopedia and a range of volumes from history and biology to a growing catalog of novels. When New York teachers went on strike in 1968, the teachers taught free at the local synagogue, so kids would not fall behind. Parents of all religions sent their kids. They took us on numerous field trips. I saw *One Flew over the Cuckoo's Nest* on (off-) Broadway. I saw my favorite team, the Cincinnati Reds, play the Mets at Shea Stadium, and met Reds catcher Johnny Edwards at the gate after the game. And we visited the Museum of Modern Art. For a group of very young Brooklyn kids, the near universal reaction to Pablo Picasso's *Guernica* was *WTF*. Except of course for the two or three insufferable teacher's pets who did their homework and insisted they could dissect the painting's aesthetics and politics.

This time, in Madrid's storied museum of 20th-century art, named for Queen Sofia, I am shaken by its emotional content. The horror, the terror from above, the shock, the brutality, the political violence.

The German Luftwaffe wanted to test bombs and Blitzkrieg tactics, and the efficacy of terror from the skies. The Basque town of Guernica was leveled. It was April 26, 1937, and the fascist alliance between Franco, Hitler, and Mussolini was an urgent prelude to the coming conflict that would end 75 million lives.

I stand watching awhile and study the reaction of the museum's large crowd, gathered to honor an iconic Spanish master. I am heartened. These days at tourist destinations, people shoot selfies and wander to the next Insta-ready photo opp. Not here. There is an atmosphere of solemnity, of awe and respect. No chattering. No checking phones. I ask the security lady if it's OK to take photos without flash. She rolls her eyes and nods toward the crowd. Ah, I see, people taking photos. Got it. I like the fact that most Spanish staff refuse to speak English. Inconvenient for me, but always good to strike a blow against cultural hegemony.

I wander down to the cafeteria after a first viewing. It's easy to get lost in Reina Sofia's multiple towers. The cafeteria is magnificent, a gorgeous splash of modernist color and comfortable, artfully designed seats. I order a citrus salad and sparking water, the healthiest meal I have had since touching down in Lisbon. And I read about *Guernica*.

Picasso did not do political art till that point. But his lover, surrealist photographer and anti-fascist activist Dora Maar, urged him to paint it. Maar exhibited with Salvador Dali and Man Ray and was a signatory to Andre Breton's '*appel à la lutte*', a 1934 call for intellectuals to fight the gathering threat of fascism. *Guernica* was commissioned by the Spanish Republic for display at the 1937 Paris International Exposition. To the public expo-goer unfamiliar with Cubist art, the reaction was akin to my Brooklyn comrades. *What. The. Actual…*

I appreciate the consistency of Euro payment methods; I have not used cash since arriving. I pay my bill and wander back up to *Guernica* for a fresh second look. In the next room is the art of the anti-fascist Republic. The aesthetic of the posters and flyers is inciting and confident. Liberty and a new world are yours to seize, your birthright as Spaniards. These were not shy people. They saw the threat and named it, unconcerned with the exigencies of academic precision.

Fascism.

There are printed pamphlets and newspapers and periodicals in glass covered displays, along with the posters adorning a large wall. The internecine conflicts, which would hamper if not doom the anti-Franco effort, between Stalinists, Trotskyites, social democrats, government loyalists, unionists, and anarchists are woven through the imagery. I take some photos for sharing with project followers, one capturing a wide view of both the room's anti-fascist propaganda and the *Guernica* painting in the adjoining space. I will spend the evening rereading George Orwell's *Homage to Catalonia*. The Brit, whose *1984* and *Animal Farm* are, along with Aldous Huxley's *Brave New World*, the most-read indictments of totalitarianism, went to Spain to put his life on the line to join the resistance against Franco. His focus on the destructive infighting and subversion by Soviet agents has been the subject of controversial and diverging analyses. He traveled far to join the fight, got a bullet in his neck for his effort, then was hunted and almost murdered by Stalinist cadres who deemed his POUM militia not sufficiently revolutionary.

This second visit to *Guernica* allows a closer look at the detail. The mother and baby, the use of bull and horse likenesses. The light from above along with the man holding the gas light. The wanton destruction and terror. I don't have the art history credentials to understand the esoteric imagery or Cubist forms but there is a visceral impact. In a room nearby is a set of 'postscripts', the women of *Guernica,* a series of related art pieces. Viewing these smaller bits offers context and fullness to what I see in the main room. And that leads me to wander through the museum. Ah, here is Dali's masturbation painting, along with psychedelic renderings that seem impossible to imagine without hallucinogens. I enjoy and appreciate walking the rooms and take what I can in my own way. I love wandering through grand structures holding grand ideas, libraries and bookstores, cathedrals, museums, monuments.

After my wander, I navigate the towers and halls for a final look at *Guernica.* This time, I am impressed by the sheer scale, the audacious vision, the translation of political messaging and reportage to a singular creative vision on a very large canvas. My friend Chaun is surprised when I send him photos of my visit. He remembers it as having more color. Yes, Picasso affected that. The grey, black, and white coloring, on a canvas 11 feet 5 inches tall and 25 feet 6 inches across, is meant to evoke the dust and ash left after the bombing and the suffering wrought by violence and chaos.

I want to visit the nearby Prado museum but there is no time. I head back to the hotel to pack and prepare for my train ride to Barcelona.

A Short History of the Regime of Francisco Franco

Spain experienced high unemployment, inflation, and social unrest in the aftermath of World War I. These problems were exacerbated by political instability and the ineffectiveness of the parliamentary system.

1923: General Miguel Primo de Rivera leads a coup that establishes a military dictatorship, with the support of King Alfonso XIII, to 'restore order' in the country. His regime suppresses political freedom but fails to solve Spain's economic and social problems.

1930: Primo de Rivera resigns, and the monarchy attempts to restore constitutional rule. The return to parliamentary democracy in 1931 sees the establishment of the Second Republic, marked by deep social divisions and political polarization.

1931-1933: The new republican government introduces significant reforms, including land redistribution, secularization, and military restructuring. These reforms alienate conservatives, the military, and the Catholic Church. The rise of left-wing parties, including socialists and anarchists, lead to a backlash from the right, resulting in political violence and the formation of fascist groups like the Falange Española, founded in 1933 by José Antonio Primo de Rivera.

1934-1936: The conservative CEDA (Spanish Confederation of Autonomous Right-wing Groups) briefly takes power, reversing many republican reforms. The political situation deteriorates further, with widespread strikes, riots, and assassinations.

1936: The Popular Front, a left-wing coalition, wins the general elections. In response, a group of military officers, led by General

Francisco Franco, launch a coup on July 17, 1936, initiating the Spanish Civil War. Franco receives military aid from fascist Italy and Nazi Germany, while the Soviet Union supports the Republicans. Western democracies hesitate to allow arms shipments or otherwise support the forces of the republic against the fascist alliance. Franco's Nationalist forces win the war in 1939, leading to the establishment of a dictatorship.

1939-1975: After the Nationalist victory, Franco establishes an authoritarian regime and competing political parties are banned. Franco rules by decree. The judiciary is purged of republic supporters and special courts are established to try political opponents. The regime uses the courts to silence dissent and solidify control.

Franco pursues autarky (economic self-sufficiency), which leads to economic stagnation and widespread poverty. It was not until the 1950s and 1960s, with the adoption of more liberal economic policies, that Spain begins to experience economic growth, although the benefits are unevenly distributed.

1942: A new rubber-stamp parliament, the Cortes Españolas, which has no real power, is controlled by Franco. This ensures that all legislative authority remains with him, consolidating his dictatorship.

1975: Franco dies after nearly four decades of rule, and Spain transitions to democracy with the approval of a new constitution in 1978.

ADAM HOCHSCHILD
The Global Battleground

Adam Hochschild is the author of eleven books. My world view was dramatically altered a quarter century ago by my reading of his *King Leopold's Ghost: A Story of Greed, Terror and Heroism in Colonial Africa*. He is the author of *Spain in Our Hearts: Americans in the Spanish Civil War, 1936-1939*, published in 2016. In his storied career, he also served as a reporter for the *San Francisco Chronicle*, a commentator on National Public Radio's *All Things Considered*, and a co-founder, editor, and writer at *Mother Jones* magazine. He has received the Theodore Roosevelt-Woodrow Wilson Award from the American Historical Association and was elected a fellow of the American Academy of Arts and Sciences.

BG: *You spent a lot of time in the book covering the international brigades, especially the U.S. brigades and Orwell. What were they all resisting? Yes, Franco and the Nationalist army, but what idea were they resisting, what was their political fight?*

AH: I think Lincoln volunteer Maury Colow, whom I quote in my book, said it best: "For us it wasn't Franco. It was always Hitler." Millions of people all over the world were worried about the spread of fascism. But only in Spain was there a place where you could volunteer to go and fight against it.

BG: *What is fascism? And in what way does Franco qualify?*

AH: Historians differ about this. Many don't call Franco—or Salazar, in Portugal—fascist. After all, the Spanish fascist party was only one of several groups Franco welded together into his movement. But certainly Franco's regime, like Mussolini's and Hitler's, was a dictatorship—and a ruthless, authoritarian one.

Unlike Mussolini and Hitler, though, his regime was tightly entwined with the Catholic Church, whose hierarchy in Spain had long been deeply right-wing.

BG: *Part of the story of those times and certainly part of Orwell's story was of the various leftist factions. In* Spain in our Hearts, *you talk about the predominance of communists among the Americans who went over, and you wrote, 'We cannot understand them without understanding why communism then had such a powerful appeal'. Americans think of communism in its Marxist-Leninist, Soviet/ Maoist incarnations. What did communism mean to those boys who went over to fight?*

AH: To them, I think, the Communist Party was a group that militantly supported labor, and that was bold enough (after getting the OK from Stalin) to organize volunteers from all over the world to go fight in Spain. No one else was doing something for Spain on that scale. The Soviet Union seemed far away, and with few exceptions (several of whom figure in my book), few Americans who went to Spain had ever been to the USSR or had much idea of what was really going on there.

BG: *More than 6,000 clergy were murdered by Republic supporters. How important was the participation of the Spanish (Catholic) Church in justifying both colonial and pre-Republic oppression, and what accounts for the rage that led to so many killings?*

AH: The Catholic Church in Spain was seen by almost everyone as an integral part of the existing power structure, closely allied with big business, the big rural landowners, and the colonial regime in North Africa. It was deeply hostile to labor unions and the left, and so clergy became a target when those tensions in Spain boiled up into civil war.

BG: *Americans today do not have the grievances that Germans had post-WWI or the economic and political challenges faced by Italians when they embraced Mussolini. What is the appeal of authoritarians in the U.S, and how do you account for the continued appeal of Donald Trump?*

AH: That's a big one! But I do think that one similarity between many Trump enthusiasts and the groups that embraced fascism in Europe in the '30s is that they feel left behind. They tend to disproportionately come from smaller towns and rural areas that have not shared in the tech boom, or that had industries that have lost jobs, like coal mining. And they're on the losing end, very often, of the huge and growing income disparities in the U.S. And then along comes a savior who says, "I can tell you who to blame."

BG: *In 'Exterminate All the Brutes', Sven Lindqvist suggests (the phrase comes from Joseph Conrad's* Heart of Darkness *about the Belgian rape of the Congo, subject of Hochschild's* King Leopold's Ghost*) that years of colonial brutality laid the moral foundation for, desensitized cultures to, brutality on the European continent. Do you agree with that notion?*

AH: I think there's some truth in what he says. But human beings in so many different societies at so many different times have shown the capacity to be incredibly cruel to each other. So I'm wary of blaming it all on one source. There was warfare and slavery in Africa, for example, before the Europeans got there.

BG: *You describe in your book past fascist movements in the U.S, such as the 20,000 who joined the Order of the Black Shirts, the American Fascisti. Is some uniquely American flavor of fascism a longstanding trend or tradition in the country's politics?*

AH: I think it's amazing that we *didn't* have a strong fascist movement in the U.S. in the 1930s. I ascribe that at least in part to

Franklin D. Roosevelt. But we certainly have a long tradition of somewhat similar things—the Klan, for example.

BG: *Back to November! What would you expect in a second Trump term?*

AH: Much trouble. It will be far worse than the first term. He'll appoint more extreme people at all levels. The Heritage Foundation is already drawing up lists for him. And he has a more powerful motive than ever for wanting to stay in power, because otherwise he's got several cases against him that may send him to jail.

BG: *Spanish fighters against fascism declared, 'No pasarán'. What should American lovers of liberal democracy be declaring or doing between now and November?*

AH: They should be out there knocking on doors, raising money, writing letters, doing everything possible to make people feel the urgency of what we're up against.

CARLOS SARDIÑA GALACHE
A Cult of Violence

Carlos Sardiña Galache was born in Madrid in 1978 and has covered Burma as a freelance journalist since 2010. His work has been published in *Al Jazeera*, the *Intercept*, the *Christian Science Monitor*, the *South China Morning Post*, *TIME*, the *Bangkok Post*, and *Nikkei Asian Review*. Author of *The Burmese Labyrinth: A History of the Rohingya Tragedy*, he translated Ian Kershaw's highly regarded biography of Adolf Hitler into Spanish.

CSG: In Spain, the label 'fascist' (*fascista* or '*facha*' in Spanish) is also used quite loosely as a slur, often inaccurately against, for instance, conservatives. Recently, the right and the far-right are also using the word 'communist' as an insult to the left (used as synonymous of totalitarian), often against positions that could be described, at most, as social democrat.

Fascism is difficult to define. Unlike Communism, for instance, it's not really a coherent ideology, and there are many different definitions of it. I would say that fascism is a modern ideology (in the sense that is completely unique in the 20th century) that subordinates the individual to the state and defines the nation in exclusionary terms (racially and ethnically). It's usually accompanied by the cult of a strong leader that embodies the nation and its usually anti-intellectual, one could consider it a reaction against liberalism and the rationality of the enlightenment (you can say that fascism is the heir of romanticism, while Marxism, in my view, is a continuation of the enlightenment project), and it stresses force with a cult of violence. Of course, it's opposed to any kind of pluralism. But I don't think fascism, when it emerged in Italy and Germany, was a movement that looks at the past, it's fundamentally a project for the future (that's why I would call it modern).

There's a somewhat heated controversy about whether the Francoist regime was fascist or not (and you can find people in the left defending it wasn't). In the strictest sense, the only organizations neatly fascist in Spain were the Falange and the Juntas de Ofensiva Nacional-Sindicalista, which ended up merging before the civil war. Franco wasn't a member of any of them. Franco was fundamentally an ultra-Catholic, authoritarian conservative, as were the other generals who staged the coup in 1936 (during the war, Franco talked about it in terms of a Holy Crusade). What he did during the civil war was to merge all the movements opposing the Republic into a single party called the 'Falange Española Tradicionalista y de las Juntas de Ofensiva Nacional Sindicalista', which included traditionalists like the Carlistas, who were not fascists at all. Of course, he supported (and was supported by)

Hitler and Mussolini, but he wasn't a fascist himself, and he tried to distance himself from them after World War Two. The Franco regime had elements of fascism (a single party, a strong statist element), of course, but it wasn't a purely fascist regime. It was more of an (extremely) authoritarian and traditionalist regime which drew its legitimacy mostly from the Catholic Church. But I understand it being labelled as fascist as a sort of shorthand.

> *Fascism is a modern ideology that subordinates the individual to the state and defines the nation in exclusionary terms, racially and ethnically.*
>
> *It's usually accompanied by the cult of a strong leader that embodies the nation and it's usually anti-intellectual.*

BG: *Did the centuries of Spanish colonial experience, and Franco after all led a colonial army in North Africa, contribute to the brutality of the Nationalists during and after the civil war?*

CSG: We must not forget that the 1936 coup that led to the civil war was staged by the so-called 'africanistas', generals who had a long career in the wars in northern Morocco. Franco was one of them. These wars, mostly in the Moroccan Rif mountain range, were extremely brutal during the first third of the 20th Century, with the Spanish military killing civilians en masse, with the use of chemical weapons and airstrikes against the civilian population in the 1920s. They were battle-hardened soldiers and officers who had fought for years against a hostile population. Except for the chemical weapons, Franco and his men took many of the tactics deployed in northern Africa to Spain during the civil war. In a certain way, the Nationalists waged the war in Spain as a sort of internal colonial war in which they didn't hesitate to collectively punish civilians.

On the other hand, there was a certain nostalgia among those generals about the conquistadores of the old times and the accomplishments of the old empire Spain lost in the 19th Century. The ideological underpinnings of that empire were, of course, deeply Catholic. The Spanish empire was, among other things, a mission to bring Catholicism to the whole world. Unlike Hitler, Franco didn't have much expansionist ambitions (he was realistic enough to realize Spain just wasn't strong enough), but there are some remnants in his rhetoric of that past. As mentioned earlier, he saw the war as a crusade against godless communists and, during the dictatorship, he would refer to Spain as the 'reserva espiritual de occidente', and the education system and state-sanctioned culture during the Francoist era used to tout the past glories of the Spanish empire.

BG: *In considering your work on Germany's embrace of Hitler and of Franco's long rule in your native country, how do you describe the current renewed enthusiasm for right wing, neo-fascist political parties in European countries like Germany and Spain?*

CSG: Until recently, Spain could boast that there was no significant far-right party, but then Vox emerged about six years ago. In reality, Vox is nothing but a faction of the Popular Party (founded by a minister of Franco, Manuel Fraga Iribarne), with some far-right elements among its ranks. I think the emergence of Vox and the far-right in Spain can be explained by the failure of the Socialist party to live up to its name (PSOE has been since the 80s closer to a Tony Blair than to its original founders), as it basically implemented neoliberal policies (privatization of state-owned companies and so on) very similar to those of Thatcher in the UK or Reagan in the U.S. PSOE basically turned to other kind of issues like gay marriage, for instance (don't get me wrong, please, I think that was great). But the economic crisis and high levels of unemployment alienated many people and PSOE didn't seem like an alternative to the neoliberal order (its economic policies since the end of the Franco have actually been not too different to those of the Popular Party). After the crisis of 2008, there was the indignados movement, and Podemos, to the left of PSOE, emerged as a viable alternative, but the seemingly endemic factionalism in the Spanish left had reduced it to a shadow of what it was. It has to be said also that the left has faced an extremely hostile media and has also been the target of an extremely conservative judiciary (incidentally, the democratic transition managed to put the military under control, but the judiciary is still Francoist to a large extent). With a neoliberal project failing, and a left discredited in the eyes of many, many people have found that the only alternative is in the far-right. The Catalonian question has also played a big role, and actually Vox got quite strengthened by it after the attempted referendum in 2017.

BG: *As a Spaniard, how have you viewed or understood the Catalan anarchist period during the Civil War? With pride? Nostalgia? What models or successes from those experiments might be useful in looking at new forms of people's governance?*

CSG: I think that was an extremely important, and interesting, political experiment which was actually suppressed by the Stalinist left. Spain is, with the possible exception of Italy, the only country in Europe where anarchism really took root, and it's still somewhat relevant. There was some of it in the *indignados'* horizontal forms of organization in 2011. Anarchism showed that it was possible for people to organize themselves, independently from the state. The whole anarchist program is probably impossible to realize, but it still provides important instruments for social self-organization and emancipation.

NICK LLOYD
Walking Barcelona

When I ask Adam Hochschild if he can suggest anyone I should meet in Barcelona, he answers, "Go see Nick Lloyd." I tell Adam we already have a date.

Nick is the author of an impressive, detailed political account of the swirl of historical dynamics driving the conflict, 'Forgotten Places: Barcelona and the Spanish Civil War', as well as a highly popular and skilled tour guide for Barcelona visitors interested in the Spanish Civil War. As a Brit, he shows remarkable empathy and understanding of the longstanding frustrations of Spaniards laboring under the injustices and violence of successive Spanish monarchs and regimes.

Our walking tour of the city starts at Plaça de Catalunya where Nick points out various landmarks—and discreet bullet holes—and describes the origins of the civil war. He has a handy chart of artifacts in his briefcase. On the left of the chart under the heading Revolution is CNT, the anarchist trade union, and Poum, the anti-Stalinist communists. On the right under Republic, is ERC, Catalan Republicans, and PC/ PSUC pro-Soviet communists. We visit hotels, bombed out plazas, scenes of atrocities, and a plaque in tribute to George Orwell, who fought for the Republic. We stopped for Catalonian hot chocolate and churros at Granja Dulcinea, named for Don Quixote's unrequited love, and had lunch at Bar Celona, a packed local favorite.

NL: It's surreal, isn't it. It all seemed a long way away. How could people do that? But then you start looking at Europe now, and there are some crazy nutters in Spain, who are not that far off from Trump. He's feeding them. He just seemed like this eccentric figure. But is he that different from Berlusconi? We've had people like him in the past in Spain, we had Jesus Gil in the 90s. Mayor of Marbella, he was like a small-town Trump. Absolutely outrageous.

Trump does seem to be on another level. Now it no longer seems so distant to be honest. Now all of those crazies have come out of the woodwork in Europe too.

BG: *Is most of it driven by the immigration issue, with perhaps a strong dose of white nationalism?*

NL: Spain had seemed to be immune to that. Had, past tense. Seemed to be the last country without an alt-right party apart from Ireland in the EU. That's changed in the last three years with the rise of Vox and fringed Vox, all of these racist ideas. Soft racism has always been there in Spain. Throwaway comments, stuff that would not be acceptable in middle class United States or the UK, silly joke type of racism. While at the same time, I don't want too many black people coming here, but I don't mind my neighbors. More like that level. When immigration became massive, in the last 20 years, that has changed. And it's not just the big cities, you go into small towns in the middle of nowhere, and you'll be served by somebody from Ukraine or Romania or from Bolivia, from Senegal, whatever. So people are fearful of change. And of course, these right-wing politicians, since that narrative has arrived through Vox, they pulled the party towards them, those more violent and more aggressive forms of racism have become real to the fore. There's a whole aura around their ideas. But at the same time, unlike other countries in Europe, Spain has as a problem because it's got one of the lowest, if not the lowest birth rate in the world. And quite simply, without immigration, the system doesn't work.

You go to the vineyards now. Everyone's from outside. And probably the guy who's running the vineyard is voting for Vox, is employing them, he needs them. But he wants to moan about them. It's really curious because the areas where Vox get the highest number of votes, these small farmers made so much money from intensive agriculture on the backs of illegally employed migrant workers. Living in shanty towns. It's medieval conditions in some of the places in the south. Almeria is the only human structure which is visible from space. It's not the Great Wall of China, you can't see that. The only visible structure is the Almeria greenhouses. You look at it on a NASA image. It's incredible. You got this little white thing at the bottom of Spain, all these green-houses. It's the area which was the poorest in Spain, one of the poorest in Europe, in the 60s, I mean African poor. And you go round these, what you might call in America, one-horse towns and there's nothing and then suddenly they're full of banks and people are buying 4x4's and there's car showrooms and some nouveau riche, and those people have voted massively for Vox, even though all their money comes from this exploitation. It's well documented.

BG: *Where are the workers coming from?*

NL: Morocco, sub-Saharan Africa.

BG: *Don't they see the paradox there?*

NL: You tell me. I don't know. But Spain does have a technical problem, at least in our current way of organizing the economy. No economy at the moment knows how to deal with a falling birthrate. Maybe we can get to the point where we can deal with a smaller population. And the world population will be smaller, in the long run, that might be a good thing. But no society knows how to do it. The only way is to import people.

BG: *And then you have this theme of Muslims and Slavs who procreate at a higher rate, who are going overwhelm our society in 50 years.*

NL: It's basically against Muslims. Which is the wonderful thing about Lamine Yamal. On the Spanish team, there are a lot of white faces. But there are two wingers, Nico William's parents escaped from, I don't know where it was, Senegal, across the Sahara, a nightmare, and ended up in Spain. Not dissimilar to Lamine Yamal's parents. He is the youngest player ever to play and score in the Euro Finals, or World Cup It's a symbol, because he's from an incredibly poor part of a town to the north of Barcelona called Mata Rome, which is relatively wealthy but has a really poor part and is one of the poorest parts of Spain. Because he's from this neighborhood, where 50 percent of the population are in risk of poverty. His goal has represented so much in the last few days for multicultural Spain. And really is sort of a slap in the face for Vox and their ideas.

The people who are the others are always gonna be different. Those who lost the civil war were the others. There are new historical memory laws and more and more investigations. Partly it's the money because there's all this research now that's come out. People have always known but it has been a bit of a taboo. What hadn't been talked about is the huge economic heist which Franco's victory represented against all those who lose the war. On a local level, like family farms, you lose that. You're a liberal doctor, either you're lucky to be alive, or you're gone, or you're dead, or you're in Mexico, and you lost your farm. And you can't do anything about it. And it's not once, it's hundreds and hundreds of thousands, if not millions of cases, and you walk around any city in Spain, you'll see in places like bars, businesses, restaurants, shops, the opening year, 1939, 1940 when Spain was in a huge economic crisis. Who opened those bars? Who had the money to open the bar in '39? How did they get the money? How did they get the bar? How did they get the license? And that's at the trivial, the low level, but of course it's also in big business. It's something like, of all the companies on the Spanish Stock Exchange, there's only a couple whose capital did not arise originally from Franco's victory in '39. The concessions they were given within that fascist regime to make as much as they wanted. One of the very few is Zara Ortega, the clothing guy, one of the richest persons in Spain. And Zara's profits, almost certainly, came from the cocaine trade in Galicia in South America. So much of Spanish capital and the big companies owe their profits to Franco's victory. Not all their profits, but all their starting capital, and that is a real threat when people start talking about that. So honoring the International Brigades, giving them citizenship, doing a documentary about anarchist cinema, remembering one guy who was a mayor who was murdered. Sponsors don't want to think on a social level. They want to think of their ancestors being heroes, not murderers. That is a threat. It's the threat of shame. And the threat of losing capital, the heist that his victory represented. And then of course that feeds into modern things, against immigration and women's rights, against Me Too, everything that's happening elsewhere. It fits nicely into all of that.

> *Of all the companies on the Spanish Stock Exchange, there's only a couple whose capital did not arise originally from Franco's victory in '39.*

BG: *It shocked me when you talked about how many clergy were killed. There was something about the Catholic Church in Spain that so enraged people, I am trying to get my head around that.*

NL: They're the figurehead, the people they talk to on a daily basis. They have so much control, not in the cities. Do you know a church in El Reval, the neighborhood next to here. Pre-war is estimated about one percent (churchgoers). This is very low. But in the countryside, they have such a power. They decide who gets to work, they decide who gets to eat, who gets to live, because if you don't work, you don't eat. Your children are hungry. Imagine the hate that would engender.

BG: *In the United States, you have Donald Trump, who does not go to church, cannot quote one Bible verse, is vulgar, cheated on all three of his wives, just lost a big lawsuit because he was fucking a porn actress while his wife had a baby and covered it up. For which his lawyer went to prison four years ago. And this guy is embraced by fundamentalist Christianity, the most powerful Christian political force in the United States, as an agent of Jesus. It's extraordinary that Christians want him in public life.*

NL: Because they want power. All they care about is power. All the compromises necessary for power. I mean, as long as we pray for his soul, he's alright anyways, isn't he? Yeah, it is extraordinary.

CHAPTER 3

FRANCE

Marseille Layover

Whereupon I stop over in Marseille on my way to Milan… meet Hazem El Moukaddem, a French Arab antifascist community leader near the Old Port, who declares the need for a new vision and celebrates the electoral defeat of French fascists… plus bullet trains, merguez, and the Travis Bickle method of safe solo travel.

HAZEM EL MOUKADDEM
"I think we are on the edge."

I meet Hazem El Moukaddem at Place Jean Jaures near Marseille's old port. The historic square is named after Socialist politician Jean Jaurès. In the 13th century, it served as a gathering place for Christian Crusaders on their way to the Holy Land. The square is ringed by outdoor tables for food and drink. A small dog bounds up to me eager for my attention. After playing with him a bit, I notice a man with a second dog, late thirties and unassuming, watching me. We introduce ourselves. Hazem suggests a walk to his favorite tea lounge for a hookah session, his two small dogs in tow. En route, numerous people approach us to greet him warmly. He is either very friendly or a community leader of some import. Or both. We settle into a back room of the lounge as Hazem ignites a hookah brought by a waitress. Lebanese by birth, his reputation as a fierce antifascist activist belies his gentle and engaging demeanor.

BG: *Start with your thoughts on the most recent French election. How serious a concern was a potential Le Pen government?*

HEM: My first thought is a sort of relief. We cannot be unhappy; we cannot be happy. The only thing we could be happy about was the National Front losing, it was about the law and Le Pen. It was a cause of stress for a lot of people, especially somewhere like Marseille, where half of the city is coming from elsewhere. And where we were expecting a really rude and really violent transition if the National Front gets the Interior Ministry, for example, which means no more papers, more controls on colored people, more controls on people with no papers, a lot of pressure on left-wing groups, a lot of pressure on progressive people. They wanted to go back on the abortion law. So yeah, it's a relief situation. It's the victory of all the people who went and voted, which is rare in France, the participation rate was really high. So to me, it's a victory of the people showing that they don't want a racist government. They don't want an extreme-right government. And they don't want Macron's government. To go deeper in the analysis will be complicated because some people who voted were liberals, center, left wing, hard left, never voted, don't have an opinion. So we could not see the people who voted that usually don't vote as an entity. It's a blend of a lot of different people. And the only thing that unites them, it's not the victory of the left, but the victory over the extreme right.

BG: *What do French supporters of Le Pen find appealing about her ideological position and promises?*

HEM: That's a very complicated question. Because like, the hard base of Le Pen are the classic racist people. Then comes the comedy that the zones where the fascists are stronger before were communist zones. And we really saw the evolution of the working class as in industrial workers, as in shitty jobs workers, going from communist party to National Front. And this is something that we need to understand and to study because, to me, it's a vote of despair. It's not a vote of logic. The communists were in these zones 10 years ago.

And you had a third part that gave a lot of dynamics to the campaign, a lot of young people follow Jordan Bardella without understanding the roots of what it is. I'm not saying they're stupid, or they don't know history, I'm saying that since they didn't live the multiple dramas of the extreme right in recent history, World War Two, to them, the Anti-Fascist or anti-racist speech or the progressive speech is just propaganda. And this is scary. When you talk to a smart, 18-year-old gay guy and he tells you, I vote National Front because the only people who attack me are Arab people, I'm like, really? You *are* Arab. It's something to work on. And to me it's a disappointment that most of the work that's been done on the National Front/ *Rassemblement National* was in a very ideological way, as opposed to trying to understand the shift that happened with the people voting for them.

BG: *Is Le Pen fascist?*

HEM: What is fascism today? I don't have a definition of what are the others, I have a definition of what I want. And I believe in a society where people should have health care, access to education, do whatever they want, in the respect of the other, be whatever they want, and be able to progress without being blocked by social structure, social pressure. And the National Front agenda, I'm saying the National Front because I don't know how to translate (the new version) Rassemblement National. Which was also a shift because they wanted people to forget what National Front is, and to make like they are a new face, but it's the same structure. Today, if you look at what the National Front votes in parliament, they vote to ban abortion. They vote to complicate the life of people who got here fleeing misery, and living in misery, and making their life even more miserable as if it changes something for them. And they think that they could handle this with authority. And maybe they can, because 90 percent of the cops, that's an official statistic, vote for them. This is scary, to know that nine cops out of 10 supports this openly racist agenda.

> *I believe in a society where people should have health care, access to education, do whatever they want, in the respect of the other, be whatever they want, and be able to progress without being blocked by social structure, social pressure.*

I'm left-wing. A big part of what was responsible of the loss of sense of what is fascism was because they were crying fascism every five minutes when the majority of society had a left-wing sense of values. And they abused it. And now the values of society are right wing. And it's becoming more and more traditionalist. And the use of the words don't have the same effect anymore. We are fighting a cultural war to win back these values. This is why the use of words should be done in a really careful way, to use the words when they need to be used, and on examples that are factual, not propagandist issues. So to me, National Front are neo- proto- fascists, whatever you want to call them, not as in the classical definition, but as an evolution in an evolved Europe. And we need to fight them on this basis. But you also need to think back about our vocabulary and to know how to use stuff. It's very simple to say they are against abortion, they are not for LGBT rights, which is very funny because they have a big LGBT voting section. And to also reinvent the sense of words.

BG: *The Command of the French Foreign Legion is a short drive from here. Is French colonial history something that people on the right yearn for, are nostalgic for, and is that manifested their attitude toward ethnic minorities?*

HEM: Yes, and no. To me, yeah, colonialism affects a lot of the behavior of today's generation in an unconscious way. Actually, it's very funny. Even on the left, you have people coming from big families, going to university, and going to poor neighborhoods telling black and Arab people how to behave (*laughs*). To me, this is a form of colonialism too. Thinking that you have the truth and the others are below you. So yeah, we live in a racist society. If you look on the left to see who got elected, how many black and Arab descendants are there? Not a lot.

I work in a kebab from time to time. And sometimes it's very funny. White people telling me, this is the first time I eat a kebab and I'm like, where are you from? And they're from Marseille and I'm like, how the fuck can you live in Marseille… you see what I mean? It's almost a rebellion for them to eat a kebab. It's like the most eaten sandwich on the streets.

BG: *What's your vision or what's the vision of the left here in Marseille as to what kind of a society, what political structures need to be built?*

HEM: I think that we are in this shitty situation because of a lack of vision. No one in the past 30 years gave hope or gave aim to go forward. We were defending what was won in the past, rather than pushing forward to advance. And this was a huge mistake. If you see most speeches today on the left, it's really about defending the past. It's not thinking about the future. This is scary, it means that we are losing, losing, losing. People are focused only on the elections, and they don't work between elections. And when they win, most of them are not here anymore. It's really sad. I think we need to rethink the whole of political activism.

BG: *Is communism at all popular these days with people that you talk to?*

HEM: They did one percent I think in the election.

BG: *These days, what does a French Communist believe?*

HEM: I'm going to be harsh. Today, Communist Party members defend only their political jobs, their city halls, their deputies, because their structure doesn't survive because people don't believe in communism but in the money coming from their elected people. You remove this, they don't exist anymore.

> *I think that we are in this shitty situation because of a lack of vision.*

BG: *What is the view that you and people on the left here in Marseille have as to the immediate future of American politics?*

HEM: Obviously, Trump is a disaster. I think the people around him are really smart and make campaigns that make a lot of sense for a part of society. And the whole program is to divide society in two.

There's a part of my society that is becoming more and more racist, in a modern way, but rooted in the World War Two values and the values of fascism. Like when I open the internet, to me it's like fucking crazy, because I see all this hate speech. I have received 1000s of insult messages, even letters to my house after an article in the extreme right newspaper. And it's hard for me to analyze this because I don't know if it's like trolls, AI, real people. I don't know if the real people who are insulting me believe in what they are saying or not, if they're not just only decompensating or decompressing. Like five or six times I met in the street, people who wrote shit about me. And I was like, hello, do we have a problem? Is this you who wrote this? I was like, hello there, I'm the guy you insulted. Do we have a problem here? And they're all like, baba, baba, bah, bah, bah, bah. And I'm like, how can you write something and see the person in front of you and behave differently? And I don't have the knowledge to answer the how and why. But a lot of people today, even the left wing are living in narratives.

The best example is my neighbor who voted National Front, and I discover his Facebook page. And I was like, wow, he's posting really racist, deep racist stuff, white people are disappearing etc., etc… You will not replace us. Yes. And I was like, fuck, and I spoke to him. And I'm like, do you believe in this shit? And he's like, no, but you see blah blah blah… and I was like, just cut it. Keep living where you're living and leave me alone. And then, this newspaper article was really interesting, because he posted it. And I was like, man, you live above me and you see me every fucking day, you know that half of it is a lie. This is crazy. And he knew it was a lie. And he posted it anyway, and he really wanted to keep and reinforce his narrative and believe in it, even if it's false. And this is something I don't touch. And I don't understand yet. And maybe I will never understand. But I think it's really interesting to study or to try to analyze, to see how come desperate people are grabbing fictional reality and trying to move forward with it. And I have like 10 or 12 funny stories like this.

BG: *That is contemporary social media. But it's also ancient, going back to the brutality with which French colonial troops treated people in Africa and various places around the world with some ideal…*

HEM: I defend this (narrative) as a militant. As in colonization, a basis of values that constructs racism and encourages people to be violent to non-white people, because to them, they are below, even if they don't express it in this way. But you have also people who don't see reality anymore, because they are absorbing propaganda all the time, all the time, all the time. And they're hanging on to fiction. And it's crazy.

I had another really funny, crazy story. I had a Marseille anti-fascist t-shirt, which in Marseille is easy to wear. And, I see two young guys, maybe 17, really skinny, looking at me, and then giving me the finger. I advanced on them. I was like, hello there, is there a problem or something? I didn't understand what the problem was. And they were like, "Run, you blue-haired homosexual left wing bitch," or something like that. They talked really badly. And I have a really violent history and I was really surprised and I was on the defensive and I was like, two young people talking to someone who has both their weight in fat and muscle and that looks really aggressive? They should have a knife or a gun or something. They should never talk like this. And they kept talking shit. And at one point, I slapped one. And he starts to cry, and the other one ran away. And I was like, fuck man, I could have punched really hard and really hurt you. Why the fuck did you talk to me like this?

BG: *They're emboldened by something. On one hand Muslims are going to replace us because they're fucking so much and having so many kids, but they're all gay.*

HEM: He was terrorized. And he told me something, this is why I'm talking about the fictional narrative. He told me, on YouTube, they say you are all gay or something. Like that. And I was like, man, look at you, look at me. You don't need to be a genius to understand that in a physical fight I will shred you to pieces. Why the fuck did you provoke me? And they were so much in their propaganda, they didn't understand that they were in reality. And to me it was scary. And it's also scary to me to see young people in here, in a left-wing neighborhood starting sometimes to take racist vocabulary. Not in a negative way. But like it's us and them. Who is us, who is them?

BG: *How concerned are you about a resurgence of fascism around the world?*

HEM: I think we're on the edge. And either we will go in the positive way or we will go in the negative way. Both scenarios are powerful. The fascist scenario is more powerful than the progressive one. Everyone lies and that's a problem because when you lie a lot, it's not about people not believing you anymore, but they don't believe in anything anymore. They don't see hope. They don't have vision. And when someone comes with true vision, they will say, he's just another one. To me grassroots, local, very local activism should be something that we look for. And I find it crazy that in here, the left gets like 89% votes left in this neighborhood. And it's crazy when our old lady gets kicked out from her house. We are coming to block that. And everyone's saying, 'You are behaving like mafioso and no one is moving grandma from her house'. So everyone is voting for the right of decent habitat. But when someone gets kicked out of a house that she lived in for 50 years, no one is defending her. How do you want her to believe in you anymore? How do you want Arab descendants or black descendants to believe in you when you talk about anti-racism all the time and there is no Arabs that are elected or black people in your list? And if they are, they are doing unimportant stuff. As if you're saying there are no immigrant descendants that are qualified.

This is the core of it. The left wing is not focusing on the people voting for them, which is crazy. They are more looking for the upper middle class central votes, thinking that the working class is already voting for them. They're not voting for you. Not anymore. They are either not voting or they are voting National Front.

> *The fascist scenario is more*
> *powerful than the progressive one.*
>
> *Everyone lies and that's a problem because*
> *when you lie a lot, it's not about people not*
> *believing you anymore, but they don't believe*
> *in anything anymore. They don't see hope.*

BG: *If you had advice for Americans, what would that be?*

HEM: It's the same advice as in the elections lately, like fuck Trump. And I know Biden is not cool. But the first move should be fuck Trump. And then if you should push it more, you should ask yourself, how come Biden is here? And why not someone else? And why is it always old people with money and not young people with vision or hope? We used to call ourselves the first line, like those who are in front. And the first frontline is, fuck Trump. And in Marseille, I heard crazy speeches, saying, yeah, but if we don't vote and Le Pen wins, maybe this will mobilize the population. You say this because you have the privilege to be safe.

BG: *And is that the culture here, you and yours assertively encouraging people to get out to vote?*

HEM: I have a special story. I came here as an immigrant. There was a true gang war with the fascists, the Nazis, the proto-fascists, who were winning. And I became an anti-fascist, not by ideology, but just because I didn't want to get beaten up. By necessity. So this is how I entered politics. And I thank all the comrades who come from different backgrounds. Who educated me and gave me access, made me speak better. Made me think better because I wasn't that progressive as a kid. I learned a lot in my life. And it's funny because I see it a lot in the left wing. They would criticize people near them. But when there's someone aggressive against them, they will be nice. This is a bad lesson in life. You should be aggressive to aggressive people. And nice to nice people.

BG: *In the short time that we walked from the park to here, you were greeted warmly by many people. Why is that? Are you just a very friendly guy, are you trusted as a community leader?*

HEM: I'm really not friendly. I started in antifascist action. We were considered as a terrorist group by the government. We were really violent towards violent people. And then thanks to the mélange, the mix between street people who are defending themselves and political people giving education, we evolved from bad boys who only think about territory to people thinking about life conditions, working conditions, neighbors. And in my lifetime, my aim is to improve the life of people around me. I don't see myself influencing the whole world or the whole country or the whole city. But in this neighborhood, I would like to work and make it clear that you will not be a victim of racism, you will not get kicked out of your house. You will not get racketeered by mafia; you will have the right to love whoever you are. And to me, that's the basis of life. I lived in the street. I know what misery is. I had no papers. I know what it is. And to me, it's almost not political. I don't want this for my worst enemy. It's like solitary prison. I don't wish this for anyone. And I have friends who've done 6-7-8 years, or 20-30 days small stretches. I wish this for no one. But there's a huge difference between I wish it for no one and if there is an aggressive person in front of me, I will walk all over him. That's something else, and we lose this in left wing.

I say there's a high criminality in Marseille and I believe that the answer is more education, more social centers, being around the young people, helping them to have jobs, helping them to discover what is community and to feel like a part of community, because left wing people see themselves outside of the community. But tomorrow, if it's an Arab kid, black kid, white kid puts his hand in my pocket or touch the ass of my friend, I will slap him. People say, oh, but the solution is education. Yeah, this is a long-term solution. But today, you have a direct problem, you need to cut it and say it's bad.

The next day I return to Place de Jean Jaurès. Jaurès was a parliamentary and philosophical leader of French socialism from the 1890s until his assassination in 1914 by a young nationalist, enraged that he advocated peace through arbitration. Cofounder of the newspaper *L'Humanité,* his *A Socialist History of the French Revolution* is considered an influential guide to political activism.

I was instructed that this might be a rough neighborhood but it feels much like lower Manhattan. Rappers, families with kids, tattooed and pierced teenagers, elders arguing sport or politics while having a smoke and a beer in the sun. Before returning to the plaza, I have brunch at a tourist-priced bistro overlooking the port then walk the area for an hour. I am impressed by the street art which also covers many storefronts, presumably with permission or at least indifference. I stop to watch two small kids on their bikes stop in front of a rapper, taking it all in. I wander over to a fellow grilling merguez, a Maghrebi sausage popularized in France by Algerian immigrants in the 1960s, made from lamb or beef or both, heavily spiced with cumin and harissa. I wait my turn. It's worth the wait.

I find myself comfortable in neighborhoods like these. And even at night, in my years of travel, I find myself unconcerned. New Yorkers are trained in the Travis Bickle method of assertive belligerence. In *Taxi Driver*, Robert DeNiro's character talks to imaginary aggressors, asking, "You talking to me?" The trick is to walk with purpose, unconcerned, and if someone is giving you an extended stare, quicken your pace, walk in their direction, and glance at them with an expression of dismissal or contempt as you pass them by. The world is a lot safer than travel guides or television dramas would have you believe.

My hotel is adjacent to the St. Charles station and I'll head out to Milan by way of Genoa via Ventimiglia in the morning. France was not on the original itinerary, but Marseille seemed a natural stopover point and I leave grateful for my encounter with Hazem. I was expecting an aggressive, provocative political posture, welcome for these times. I asked for a vision and expected something apocalyptic and revolutionary. Instead, he grounded me with a sense that human decency, social justice, access to quality health care and education, community involvement, and active political participation are universal values.

CHAPTER 4

ITALY

Mussolini's Legacy

Whereupon I blow off my train transfer in Ventimiglia to swim in the Mediterranean… discuss the history and dynamics of fascism, the appeal of Benito Mussolini, and the guardrails of democracy over a homecooked Genovese pasta and prosecco lunch in Milan with Giorgana and three prominent journalists from Italy's largest newspaper … have a chat with psychologist and political analyst Nick Carmody on the nature of personality cults and political tribalism… pay a visit to the plaza where Mussolini and his mistress were hung from their feet by antifascist partisans… how a serendipitous train stopover in Verona results in a Branzini and Negroni supper followed by an opera in a 2,000-year-old arena… and a short history of the antifascist anthem Bella Ciao.

An American friend finds it bizarre that I don't catch a $50 flight from Marseille to Milan, instead choosing a sequence of four trains over nine hours to get there. But you don't get the physical experience of the land on a flight and the project concept is to traverse the continent, encountering strangers and interesting places along the way.

I board the TGV bullet train, ensuring my Eurail app and seat assignment are intact. First class is not much more on these journeys, an upgrade to my senior global pass for the entire trip is only a hundred Euro, but it generally secures air-conditioning, a comfortable seat, electrical outlets, some breathing room, and a close by club car for food and drink. The Rail Planner app confounds me. It secures my seats for the first and final leg but not for the two connections, both of which allow a few short minutes for dashing up and down stairs for the transfer. I *think* I have the right times and tickets and trains from the Eurail app and website and emailed tickets but the instructions for multiple transfers are sometimes obscure. I don't have a strong grasp of the language in any of these countries and hubris and assertiveness gets you far, but the failure to study basic phrases in advance has its consequences.

We are late pulling into Ventimiglia, so I go the ticket window and ask for the next train to Genoa, my transfer to Milan. Better yet, I ask if I can get a first-class seat on a direct train to Milan. Nope, the 3pm is full, same for the 5pm, but the 7pm which pulls into Milan at 11 is available. I notice on the departures board that my train to Genoa has not yet left, so I go flying up the stairs and, voila, it's still there, so I jump onboard, stow my bags, and sit. There is no air-conditioning and no Wi-Fi. And it's hot. My shirt is already soaked with sweat. I will have a 12-minute window to catch my next transfer to Genoa and the train shows no sign of moving. No, I realize, it's not just hot, it's very hot. Still no movement. My brain juggles the options, the risks, the pros and cons, and I grab my bags and jump off the train, barreling back down the stairs and get to the ticket lady. Seven o'clock to Milano first class seat? Sure, and after a flurry of stamps, a printout, and a swipe of my card, it's set.

One other reason to get off here. My Vodaphone Lisbon eSIM seems to have stopped working. I thought it said I had 5 GB left, then one, then it looked like five again, and now, it's kaput. I fashion myself not dependent on my phone in my daily life but on this trip, it's a lifeline. It absolves me of most of my language-deficit sins. I can look things up, locate myself, even use a translation app in a pinch.

Sometimes I get so immersed in my MacBook Air screen on the train that I forget to check out the countryside. The hills and towns from Marseille through the south of France and into the Italian coast are varied and picturesque. And for a very long stretch, the trains run parallel to the sea. I could see the beach from the Ventimiglia train station. So I drag my Osprey Sojourn out of the station, bouncing the rollers off cobblestones and curbs.

After an eggplant parmigiana and macchiato at the café across from the station, I begin my search for a new eSIM. No one sells them. The phone store directs me to a shop across from the village church where I walk in and offer myself to be merchandised. The store sells everything from underwear to toys and indeed claims to be a Lyca mobile outlet. After a suspiciously long time inspecting my phone, the young clerk insists I am good to go, and says I should give the card an hour to activate. Unusual but, sure, and I hightail it to the beach where a nice young fellow agrees to hold my backpacks and, after a sampling of lemon Italian ices reminiscent of my Brooklyn childhood—cherry and lemon were the only flavors on offer back home—walk down to the sea. There is no sand, only rocks, so I walk as close to the surf as possible, place my Billabong flip flops next to a recognizable marker and jump in.

The water is cold but, after a minute or two of movement, it feels fine. I look around. Kids splashing with attentive parents, an instructive father, a young couple, and those magnificent rolling hills. And for the first time in some days, I can breathe and relax, with hours before my next train appointment.

The train arrives in Milan after a comfortable four-hour ride. The Ventimiglia phone card never worked so I went back to the store for a refund. "The computer is not working," was the odd explanation. Somehow the Vodaphone eSIM has started working again. I will get a new card tomorrow, as none is available at either the provincial or Milan train stations. At 11pm, the Milano Centrale station is jammed with people. Three hundred thousand bustle through here on a good day. The station was completed in 1931 as one the grand public works projects of Benito Mussolini's fascist regime. A memorial to the thousands of Jews deported from here to Auschwitz and other death camps is on a sublevel below the main tracks. Detainees arriving from San Vittore Prison between 1943 and 1945 were loaded onto livestock cars for a weeklong journey, often in bitter cold, to their almost certain deaths. In the main station concourse, a small plaque displays this line from Italian Holocaust survivor Primo Levi:

> *Bearing witness matters since*
> *everyone's anguish is our own.*

I booked my hotel with my newly alive internet connection while rolling into the station. There is a functional though frustrating dynamic in choosing lodging. In the weeks leading up to the trip, I had to focus on the Kickstarter campaign and transport and interview setup and preparation. I looked at hotels but there was a complex task locating near interviews and landmarks while synching both incoming and outgoing stations, not always the same. The priorities of hotel reviewers were helpful but not necessarily my focus. It is comforting to know your hotel is close to the station so you can just rock right over in 10 minutes. No traffic, no crossed signals with taxi drivers. And so in a big city like Milan, I picked a hotel that was a 20-minute walk from the station. It's 11pm and I am tired—I started the day in Marseille, watched the south of France speed by, swam in the Italian Mediterranean, and did a solid stretch of work on the trains. There is a long line for taxis, and I lust for exercise, so I decide to walk to the hotel. Safety is not an issue, perhaps because of my gender or demeanor or appearance—I am soaked in sweat and look an unappetizing mark for a local hood.

I am pleased to be let in by the elderly fellow at reception. I ask about breakfast and he reprimands me for not buying it in my booking. Not sure what he said but *no breakfast for you* is a likely translation. There is no elevator. There are no apparent shampoos and soaps in the room, though I find them in an odd spot on my second day. And the shower is the smallest I have ever seen. I have to wedge myself into it. But I am delighted and I have located a close by laundromat and I am clean and I slip into the bed and I dream of trains and Italian ices.

The next day, I sit in a café near the Piazzale Loreto, where Mussolini and his mistress were hung from their feet after being killed by Italian partisans on April 28 in 1945. It's a gruesome and important historic moment in modern Italian history. I look for a marker or remnant of the moment but cannot find one in this busy central thoroughfare. Instead, I sit in a café a block from Mussolini's final indignation and spend time with his *The Doctrine of Fascism*, his stern domineering stare greeting me on the cover. It's not an easy read and runs counter to all I came to embrace.

> *"Never more than at the present moment have the nations felt such a thirst for an authority, for a direction, for order. If every century has its own peculiar doctrine, there are a thousand indications that Fascism is that of the present century. That it is a doctrine of life is shown by the fact that it has created a faith; that the faith has taken possession of the mind is demonstrated by the fact that Fascism has had its fallen and its martyrs."*

I feed my Italian jazz and pop playlist into my earbuds while quaffing a Sicilian white wine and, after tunes from Paolo Conte and Lucio Dalla, up comes *Bella Ciao*. The song came to my attention by chance several months back as I began research for the trip. Something about the pathos of the rendition grabbed my attention. And it kept coming back in my playlists. I looked for a live version on YouTube and watched the scene from the hit Spanish TV series *La Casa De Papel (Money Heist)*, then the iconic Yves Montand performance.

In the morning I got up
oh bella ciao, bella ciao, bella ciao, ciao, ciao (goodbye beautiful)
In the morning I got up
To the paddy rice fields, I have to go.

And between insects and mosquitoes
oh bella ciao, bella ciao, bella ciao, ciao, ciao
and between insects and mosquitoes
a hard work I have to do.

The boss is standing with his cane
oh bella ciao, bella ciao, bella ciao, ciao, ciao
the boss is standing with his cane
and we work with our backs curved.

The origins of the song are uncertain, though it is believed to have been sung by seasonal rice field workers in Italy's Po Valley from the late 19th century onwards. They worked at *mondare*, weeding the fields to support the growth of young plants. It was an exhausting, backbreaking task, performed mostly by women known as *mondine* from the poorest social classes. They would work all day with bare feet in water up to their knees, backs bent. The difficult working conditions, long hours, and low pay led to rebellions in the early 20th century. To ensure their productivity, the master of the fields would strike them with a cane.

Oh my God, what a torment
oh bella ciao, bella ciao, bella ciao, ciao, ciao
oh my God, what a torment
as I call you every morning.

And every hour that we pass here
oh bella ciao, bella ciao, bella ciao, ciao, ciao
and every hour that we pass here
we lose our youth.

But the day will come when we all
oh bella ciao, bella ciao, bella ciao, ciao, ciao
but the day will come when we all
will work in freedom.

After World War Two, the song sprouted new lyrics to celebrate the anti-fascist partisans fighting Mussolini's government. While many believed it was sung by partisans during the war, most musicologists and historians believe its adoption as an anti-fascist anthem came later.

One theory as to the origin of the melody was identified by researcher Fausto Giovannardi, following the discovery of a Yiddish melody recorded by a Russian klezmer accordionist in 1919 in New York.

The song has grown international wings. Two Ukrainian soldiers in the trenches singing a version of the anthem was widely shared across social media. It has been recorded in numerous languages and performed by folk, world music, punk, and EDM artists as an anthem of resistance and freedom. Two Iranian women, without hijab, sang it in Farsi in response to the Islamic Republic's crackdown on protests after the death of Masha Amini in police custody. I've listened to all and the song has been an inspiration through the project. The Iranian video is a favorite.

The 'partisan' version was first published in 1953. French balladeer Montand's 1963 interpretation shot to fame after the group Il Nuovo Canzoniere Italiano performed it at the 1964 Festival dei Due Mondi at Spoleto, both as a song of the *mondine* and as a partisan hymn.

Oh partisan carry me away,
oh bella ciao, bella ciao, bella ciao, ciao, ciao
oh partisan carry me away
Because I feel death approaching.

And if I die as a partisan,
oh bella ciao, bella ciao, bella ciao, ciao, ciao
and if I die as a partisan
then you must bury me.

Bury me up in the mountain,
oh bella ciao, bella ciao, bella ciao, ciao, ciao
bury me up in the mountain
under the shade of a beautiful flower.

And all those who shall pass,
oh bella ciao, bella ciao, bella ciao, ciao, ciao
and all those who shall pass
will tell me 'what a beautiful flower'.

This is the flower of the partisan,
oh bella ciao, bella ciao, bella ciao, ciao, ciao
this is the flower of the partisan
who died for freedom.

A Short History of Benito Mussolini's Rise to Power

1919, MARCH 23: Mussolini founds the Fascist Party (Fasci Italiani di Combattimento) in Milan.

1921, MAY: Mussolini is elected to the Italian Parliament.

1921, NOVEMBER 9: The National Fascist Party (Partito Nazionale Fascista) is established.

1922, OCTOBER 27-29: The March on Rome. Mussolini and his followers stage a coup, and Mussolini is appointed Prime Minister by King Victor Emmanuel III.

1923, DECEMBER: The Acerbo Law is passed, giving the party with the most votes a two-thirds majority in Parliament.

1924, APRIL: The Fascist Party wins the elections, securing a significant majority.

1924, JUNE: Socialist leader Giacomo Matteotti is murdered, causing a political crisis.

1925, JANUARY 3: Mussolini takes responsibility for the violence and begins establishing a dictatorship.

1925, DECEMBER: Laws are passed to suppress opposition parties and the free press, solidifying Mussolini's control.

1926, NOVEMBER: Laws banning all political opposition are enacted.

1927, APRIL: The OVRA, a secret police organization, is established to suppress dissent.

1929, FEBRUARY 11: The Lateran Treaty with the Vatican is signed, recognizing the sovereignty of Vatican City and improving relations with the Catholic Church.

1935, OCTOBER: Italy invades Ethiopia, leading to international condemnation and sanctions by the League of Nations.

1936, MAY: Italy conquers Ethiopia and Mussolini proclaims the Italian Empire.

1939, MAY: The Pact of Steel is signed with Nazi Germany, strengthening the alliance.

1939, JUNE: Italy invades Albania and incorporates it into the Italian Empire.

1940, JUNE 10: Italy enters World War II on the side of the Axis Powers.

1943, JULY 9-10: Allied forces invade Sicily.

1943, JULY 25: Mussolini is deposed by the Grand Council of Fascism and arrested. King Victor Emmanuel III appoints Marshal Pietro Badoglio as Prime Minister.

1943, SEPTEMBER 3: Italy signs an armistice with the Allies.

1943, SEPTEMBER 12: Mussolini is rescued by German forces and installed as the head of the Italian Social Republic in Northern Italy, a puppet state of Nazi Germany.

1945, APRIL 25: The Italian resistance movement stages a major uprising in Northern Italy.

1945, APRIL 27: Mussolini is captured by Italian partisans while trying to escape to Switzerland.

1945, APRIL 28: Mussolini is executed by partisans in Giulino di Mezzegra.

1946, JUNE 2: Italians vote in a referendum to abolish the monarchy and establish a republic.

1947, JANUARY 1: The new Italian Constitution comes into effect, establishing a democratic republic.

PAOLO, MASSIMO, AND ANTONIO
The Pasta and Prosecco Summit

Today, I take the Metro for a Genoan lunch at the home of Paolo and Georgina Salom. I am early so I stop off at a café for an espresso and an Italian pastry. It's important to stay healthy and fit in a monthly tear across nine countries but life is short and each national cuisine demands my attention.

Paolo Salom is a longtime journalist and editor of Italy's largest newspaper, *Corriere della Sera*. He is the author of *Un Embreo in Camicia Nero, A Jew in a Black Shirt*, a chronicle of his family's experience under Mussolini's rule.

Massimo Rebotti is senior editor at the *Corriere's* political desk, an expert on Italian politics and the resurgence of the far right.

Antonio Carioti works at the newspaper's cultural desk and is a renowned author of historical books and essays, many focused on fascism, both past and current day.

As each guest arrives, important observations on Italian politics are casually shared, so I rush to assemble and activate my recording devices. I grew up in a Brooklyn neighborhood with

Italian neighbors and I'm immediately comfortable with everyone talking over each other. Each is steeped in Italian history and Mussolini's fascism doctrine and each has written extensively on the subject, including several published works.

Everyone but me brings a bottle of wine and the prosecco is opened early and I am instructed on the Genoan roots of today's multi-course pasta summit. I begin with a question to Paolo as the first course is served. Antonio apologizes for the state of his English and Paolo acts as frequent interpreter.

BG: *Paulo pointed out before lunch that Italy invented fascism, so for you, as Italian journalists and political thinkers, what is fascism?*

AC: You have to distinguish between a fascist movement and a fascist regime. In the movement, you have this aspiration to dominate the Italian political world, the political life system. When fascism was institutionalized, it had come to terms with other institutions such as the church, economic powers, and also maybe syndicates, the worker's union. Those unions that were there before were crushed, they were eliminated. Then fascism built a sort of internal union, like China's union or the Soviet Union. They were fascist unions. The idea was to create a third way between capitalism and communism, and the name they invented for this new reality economic system was *corporate activismo*. The idea was that all these spheres in the economic life of the country, industrial, education and so on, had to be subjected to the authority of the state. So, you had those *corporazioni* of builders, corporation of pharmacists, of teachers, this is something that came from the medieval time. You have the street where you have the people who sew, you had the street where you found the butcher's, the gold jewelry workers and so on. And this is something that fascism brought again into life.

BG: *It's something other than business corporations as we know them now.*

PS: It's the opposite. It's not the English meaning. It's not corporate business. No. It's what you did. You were identified by your profession. And you were bound to stick with all your federal workers and to obey certain rules set by the state.

BG: *Were these changes meeting opposition when that initial wave of reorganization was taking place?*

AC: Corporatism was realized in 1934 when fascism was already in full power. The only opposition Mussolini encountered was at the beginning of his regime when he started to shrink the freedom of society. In 1924, a deputy named Giacomo Matteotti, an elected socialist at the Chamber, was killed. He was kidnapped, beaten, and stabbed. They found his body after a few weeks. This was a real scandal in Italy. But Mussolini, instead of trying to hide what happened, made a famous speech in which he said, if you say that fascists were responsible for what happened, since I'm the chief of the fascist movement, I am responsible, I bear all the responsibility. And that is the moment when fascism shows its real face. Institutionalized violence, and everything changed from that moment on.

> *And that is the moment when fascism shows its real face, institutionalized violence, and everything changed from that moment on.*

BG: *Your Prime Minister* (Giorgia Meloni) *has some history with fascist-oriented student groups and political organizations.*

AC and **PS:** She nominated some people in the public TV system, people who belong to her faction. And the fear is that these people could transform information into a tool for the government. But if I can say, this is not fascism. When you've risen to power, you try to put your men and women everywhere you can. The difference here, Antonio says, it's not about the spoils system, which has been used, but the fact that in the past, these posts were divided into government and opposition. So there was a certain balance between all the political forces, which is now a little bit strained and it tends to be in favor of the government part.

AC: If the question is, is there a danger of fascism returning today in Italy, the answer is no. In 1919, the Fascist Party was born as a military organization, armed and violent. And Italy was just coming out of the First World War, and Italy was on its knees. In those times, society was addicted to violence. Something that today is not present at all. So, a few days after the founding of the (*Fasci Italiani di*) *Combattimento*, which is the name of these organized thugs, Mussolini ordered to set the *L'Avanti* newspaper on fire. It was his own newspaper before changing. He was a socialist journalist. He was the editor; it was the state organ of the Socialist Party. And he ordered these thugs to destroy the building, so they set it on fire. And this was the first act of an organization that was born in violent forms. And it carried from the beginning this trait, they didn't discuss the opposition, from the start, they wanted to crush it.

The great fear in those times was that after the Soviet revolution, the communists and the socialists could import the revolution to Italy. And so all the riots that were taking place in Italy after the end of the First World War, the dominant class, the industrialists, and also the middle class, their fear enabled the fascist thugs to do their work with a certain dose of appreciation from this part of society.

BG: *You say one of the distinguishing characteristics of fascism is institutionalized violence.*

AC: They attacked municipal institutions and little towns where the Socialists were in power, mayors and so on. They set all the buildings where the unions and the opposition party were located on fire. They attacked and beat to a pulp all the individuals who were linked to the opposition parties, and were leaders, local leaders, union leaders. Violence spread everywhere in the country. And it was something that the government wasn't so keen on opposing. It was tolerated.

> *They didn't discuss the opposition, from the start, they wanted to crush it.*

BG: *Four years ago during the presidential debate, Biden mentioned the Proud Boys, a right-wing militia group, almost as an insult that Trump is associated with these people, meets with these people. And Trump, instead of refuting, said, "Proud Boys, stand down and stand by," which was extraordinary. And of course, on January 6, they stopped standing by and there was a violent assault on the Capitol. For you as Italians and as students of history, how did you react to that? Did that seem familiar to you at all?*

MR: I think that violence in politics, it's nowadays a problem more in the United States than Italy. The question is, which kind of right is this right that rules in Italy? This is a question. And is it a right similar to the Tories in Great Britain or is it a right similar to Viktor Orbán in Hungary, for example. This is now our argument, our problem. But if you ask that violence is around the corner in Italy, I agree with Paolo and Antonio, no.

BG: *But do you think as you observe the United States that violence may very well be around the corner there?*

MR: Yes, I am not American. I am very interested about American affairs. I think, yes. I read, I watch that violence in politics is in the air.

In the 70s in Italy, we had a terrorism, very popular and we had lots of murders. In the current times, we see only a few episodes that police use a little bit of violence against protesters. But we don't see violence in the street about politics. I think the question for Italy is another one, which kind of right do we have?

BG: *When you say one type of right is Viktor Orbán, what does he and his regime represent to you as an Italian?*

MR: I don't know if fascism is the right word, I think that authoritarianism is the right word. And there are lots of people that like a strongman. This kind of modern fascism is very popular. In Italy, it's a little bit controversial, but the model, you can ask why Putin, for example, is very appreciated on the right. Simple decisions, short, quickly. And so I think that Orbán turns their democracy to a new form, an authoritarian democracy.

BG: *He calls it illiberal democracy, riffing on a phrase used by Fareed Zakaria.*

MR: He wins the election, but he reduces the space for the opposition, and opposition in the media. He speaks about law and order in the country and immigration. His kind of solutions are appreciated in a part of society. And the right win for this reason, in my opinion.

BG: *Democracy is a relatively new historical phenomenon. You've had a few 100,000 years of tribes and countries and feudal systems and monarchies controlled by a strongman. Is there something in human nature or in human psychology that is attracted to that kind of a figure? And is impatient with the messiness of liberal democracy?*

MR: I think this. You want to live safe and secure. And as you know, in the cities the right has more difficulties. And outside the cities they run very fast. Because I think that the people in the urban context are more educated but are more used to facing the difficulties. If you have a fear in the city, you can face this fear well. Outside, in the country, you could think about how the future could be dark. And the right is more efficient on these issues. And so this is the reason that when populist authoritarianism loses, you think, oh, it's the end. And it's never the end. Trump, when he lost, I thought it is the end.

PS: You asked about the nuances, the similarities between the U.S. situation when Trump sent his Proud Boys. And the birth of fascism in this way. There are some similarities. And some things that are not similar at all.

Now, first of all, history doesn't repeat itself. When it does, it's sort of a tragedy or some other karmic situation. When fascism was born in Italy, we had a country that had lost a lot of young men, a whole generation, 600,000 people in the First World War, our economy was shattered. The society was torn into pieces and into opposing factions. And we had the Soviet revolution that inspired a lot of people, millions everywhere, rightly so. Even today, there are people whose hearts belong to the Soviet revolution. So, fascism was born in that particular situation in Italy, in that moment. In a liberal society with only 50 years of history, because Italy was united in 1861. The government, society's fabric was thin, was not ready to face such problems. Look at the United States today, you have something very, very similar to what happened in Italy. The Proud Boys are the same thugs that you can trace to the history books in Italy. But what did they accomplish? They ruined the capitol. They made a few people die. They went to prison. You see that history repeats itself.

BG: *But if I may say, if a few small things had gone right for Trump, there would have been a very different outcome.*

PS: Of course. Yeah, but it didn't go that way. What does that mean? That the institutions are strong? That's the difference. When you find strong institutions, fascism has no place to be. It can be fought.

BG: *Wouldn't you also agree that there are in the United States and else-where economic interests, political forces that are trying to break down those institutional safeguards and that over time might be successful?*

PS: It could be. But I would make another suggestion. You have to compare today's United States to the Roman Empire. The strongest force in the world at the moment. And look at the history of emperors. Rome went through Caligula, went through Nero, and other fools. Nero even set Rome on fire. Caligula exterminated his family and beyond. But the Roman Empire was untouched. Yes, they had civil wars. Yes, they had problems. But they still stayed as the most powerful state in the world until the fourth century, and then the Byzantine Empire, which was the eastern empire when they split into two, ruled until the 16th century. So that's what I wanted to say. You can have problems. You will certainly have someone who will do anything he can to change the regime, to destroy democracy, or the way it is interpreted today. But the United States will stay what it is because it is powerful. The people are capable of eating every day. They become richer and richer. Even now, which is a terrible moment in history. So I don't think that these kinds of people can change it.

BG: *How would you describe Trump's political profile as Italians, steeped in Italian history?*

PS: Yes. As always, Italy comes first. We had Berlusconi, and Trump learned from him.

BG: *What did he learn?*

PS: That image is all.

MR: Simple message, a very simple message. And we live in a society that likes a simple message. I didn't agree with Paulo in points. I think that democracy all over the world is a little bit in crisis.

PS: I said that in the U.S. it is strong. The institutions.

I ask Paolo for a water refill and he stares at me a moment.

PS: You want water or prosecco?

I'm acculturating. Both, surely.

MR: We have a problem with democracy. I think that other types of governments, authoritarian, are more powerful and efficient at this moment. More attractive. We see new countries like China or Turkey or Russia. And that model has in Europe, for example, and in the United States some fans. I think it's not a good moment for democracy all over the world, compared to 30 or 40 years ago. Now, we have another model and is this model more efficient? I don't think so. But looks like an efficient model to face the contradictions of this era. And I think this is a big problem. In Italy, we see little pieces about this big argument. But we see also an interest, for example, Georgia Meloni is very good to do one thing. She rules for two years but she looks like the opposition, she look likes an underdog. She doesn't seem like a Prime Minister. She is very popular, because part of the people thought that she's outside the system. And I think that Trump is, Berlusconi also, when he was the president, he goes against the system, but he IS the system. This is a skill for the right.

BG: *When Trump says things like, "Only I can solve your problems," does that sound suspiciously like your fellow in the 1930s?*

PS: Yes, it's a real danger. But you have the institutions. Even if in America, you had a lot of people who would prefer fascism to democracy right now, as they did in the 30s, because Mussolini was much appreciated in the U.S. Then, yes, you could have people in the U.S. who believe that democracy is something that we have to get rid of, but after four years, he will have to go, because this is what the constitution says.

BG: *But he sure didn't want to go after his first four years. And now, he's learned a hell of a lot. So that the clumsy way that he tried to stay in power might be a little less clumsy.*

PS: I bet the Republicans will prevent this from happening.

BG: *They didn't prevent it four years ago.*

PS: They did. Pence did.

BG: *That's true, then met the fury of Republicans who denounced him as a traitor. There were a lot of Republicans, as you know, who voted against authorizing the transfer of power.*

PS: In China, now we have Xi Jinping, who changed the rules, even they have rules. You know, they have the rule which stated that the China leaders would only be in power for 10 years altogether. Five plus five. Then Xi Jinping came along. And he changed that rule and he's in power. He will be for 15 years consecutively, and probably longer, if he doesn't die before. A lot of people thought well, one day I could be president of China, they had no chance. So what will Vance do when the term will expire? Will he say okay, Trump stay in power all your life. Or will he say, I could stand a chance so go home. This is the nature of democracy, the struggle beneath.

BG: *Americans take credit for democracy, but many other countries had democratic experiments. Rome had the Senate. Do you pride yourselves on having democratic traditions?*

AC: You have to think of Rome before the Empire when it was a republic. This was a century before Christ. Until Caesar. And in those times you had a political life which was dominated by the great families, agricultural families, the power then was in the land, the more land you had, the more power you were entitled to. And when conflicts arose from interests, you had civil war. Then Rome turned into an empire, and you had votes in those times also. The Senate, for instance. Different posts in the administration were up for the vote. But the reality of it was that the regime was an authoritarian regime where a little bunch of people had all the power. The emperor was on top of that. And there was some kind of democratic turnover. But in reality, it was not a democracy, as we see today, even in Greece, the place where democracy was born. Democracy was only for people who had affluence and status.

BG: *Which was largely the case in the founding of the United States as well. Government of, by, and for the people, as long as you're male, white, and own property. Is it cynical to argue that most places in the world, through human history, are oligarchies of sorts, that people with wealth and power generally want more concentrated wealth and power?*

AC: From what I see, what you say is perfect, but the difference is on the participation of the people, the difference from the past is that you have the elevator to power which people did not have before.

PS: This is the strength of the United States. In Rome they talk about uomo nuovos, the new man. You have new men everywhere. We don't. Uomo nuovos is Vannacci, who was the general Antonio was speaking about. Who is an idiot. A complete idiot. Of course he is a general. He has no culture, but he has a lot of appeal to the public. And in fact he had 500,000 votes.

MR: He speaks about fascism.

PS: Because he is a fascist, he likes fascism. But he has no education, no real understanding of history. He has no skills. Prime Minister Meloni said important things after young people in her party cry out loud their love for fascism. They were of course, as always happens in these cases, against Jews, the scapegoats of history. And she said, these people have no place in our party.

MR: Meloni has done agreements with some countries in the north of Africa to reduce migration. She made an agreement with Albania, a new type of agreement, Italy built two bases in Albania to take the migrants, and Europe before the elections looked to this kind of solution with interest. So, Meloni doesn't say violent words, animals or something like that, against migrants. She is careful. Trump for example used violent language. She makes these agreements to take the migrants off. But for example, in Lombardy or Veneto, two of the most developed regions in Italy, the industries ask for more migrants for work but the government didn't allow this request. In other places in Italy we see very bad work conditions for the migrants. Violence, very, very low salaries, and so on. It is not the priority at the moment. It was the priority. It was an argument for the right, when the left ruled. Now, the right rule, it's not a big priority.

> *But the reality of it was an authoritarian regime where a little bunch of people had all the power. The emperor was on top of that. Democracy was only for people who had affluence and status.*

BG: *Let's go back to Mussolini for a moment. When you think because of his history as a journalist, as a socialist, what was his motivation when he came to power?*

AC: Mussolini was driven by a huge mission. He was very popular. The Socialist Party was one of the most prominent, he was one of the people who were bound to become someone in the political system in Italy. But along with this personal ambition, he thought that after the First World War, that Italy was to be a great country, not because of its present, but because of its past, the Roman Empire. He thought that democracies were weak and destined to decadence. He said that more than 100 years ago, that France and Great Britain became moot because they have fewer children than Italians did. The same as today. The modernity Mussolini was seeking had nothing to do with democracy, because he despised democracies, and the electoral system. And he thought that the way to bring the masses into the life of a nation was not through elections, but through the molding of the masses into a political body. He wanted to transform the masses, the people into something that could be useful by carrying them into the system by force, not by choice.

BG: *I'm reading Mussolini's book,* The Doctrine of Fascism. *And as an American, groomed on the idea of individual rights, it doesn't compute to me. There are no 'inalienable' or natural individual rights. There's no individual without the state. It's hard for me to understand how that could be embraced. The average Italian on the street says, 'OK, sure, I am nothing without the state?'*

AC: Mussolini was very much influenced by his experience in war. He was in the First World War, he was wounded. When you're a soldier, you have to obey your superiors, you're nothing, you're just a tool in their hands. And above all, the importance of life is obliterated. You don't have the value of life. You have to obey orders until the end. Life as such as an individual experience, it disappears into the mass of the trenches where thousands of young soldiers were kept. And they had to attack the enemy like they were nothing. Just weapons in human shape. And so, he was very much influenced by this, and violence was the only way to express this balance of power. In Italy, legally, even after the unification, people were not used to participating in the political life of a nation, only those who could demonstrate to have the ability to write and read could vote; not only that, they also had to be affluent, it was only a right for certain people. In Italy, authoritarianism was very high in those years. Only a few people really participated in political life. So the universal suffrage, the universal right to vote only for men came just a few years before the First World War, and it was abolished a few years after when Mussolini took power.

BG: *So it was easy to dismiss it. What role did colonialism play?*

AC: What I said before, he looked to the past, he wanted to change the Italian people into a nation of warriors to dominate the Mediterranean, to revive the lost, the weakness of the Roman Empire. He came late in the colonial conquest, in 1935 he attacked Ethiopia, which was part of a society of nations (League of Nations) at the time. It was a free country. Because he wanted Italy to become the kind of colonial power as other great countries like Great Britain, France, and so on. In a time where colonialism was on the verge of collapsing. So he came late. We had already conquered Eritrea. Libya in 1911. But Ethiopia was the last adventure, it was the last nail in the coffin of the regime. Because Italy lost a lot of people, a lot of men, a lot of resources.

BG: *Was any aspect of racial philosophy of Romans, of Italians racially being pure and elevated and superior? I know right at the Milano*

Central Station, there were Jews that were shipped out to concentration camps, maybe influenced by Germany at that point.

PS: Race was not as important as it was for the Germans. He once said that the blonde Nazis only think about race, because Italians in a sense felt they were different from the Germans. But after a few years, he started to use the idea that Italians were Aryans. It was important for them to demonstrate their status in Africa. But he didn't have anything against Jews until 1938. When I talked about the start of the downfall of Mussolini, when he promulgated the race laws in Italy, and anti-Jewish law, it was 1938 and, by that time, he was already a client of Hitler's. He was no longer the master; he was no longer the teacher. He depended on Germany.

BG: *Was there anything all these years later that you admire about Mussolini?*

PS: I am a Jew. To me he's a monster. Period.

AC: I said that Mussolini was a great communicator. So he was deeply loved at the time. And some of this love still persists today. And there are people who see him as somehow, well, he's done something good. Because he was really able to talk to people in a very profound way. He was in touch with the people. And you have Trump so you understand what I say. And we had Berlusconi after him. Berlusconi is a complete idiot. But there are a lot of people who see him as a great man, a great communicator. But when he was prime minister, and he had the majority of the parliament, he did nothing. So Mussolini, maybe he transformed Italy in these years, Italy seemed to be stable, rich, but it wasn't. And all the problems that Italy really had persevered when Mussolini went out. So yes, there are people who look at him as a man that somehow did something good.

MR: This is not my opinion. But I think that it's an opinion in Italy, that Mussolini is considered, exactly for the reason you asked before, the state. And we have an idea that in Italy, there is an idea that in that period, there was a strong state for the people. Houses, streets. True or false? But it's a mythical idea about that past.

BG: *Hitler and Mussolini had some grand public works projects that were very visible, that people looked at as progress.*

MR: Yes. I had a communist grandmother. She said, Mussolini made the houses for the poor people in Italy. It was right, more or less. But were lots of other things. She said bad things about Mussolini. But she remembered that house, and then about the state we have nowadays. We think we have a state that doesn't give services to the citizens. And so, in a part of society, we think at the mythical past that the state gave to the citizens, instead of liberties for example, give to the citizens services, and they improve.

There is a town in the center of Italy. The name is Latina. The ancient name is Littoria. Mussolini made that town. And in that part of Italy an idea of that mythical past remains. This town was founded in 1932. So in 2032, it's one century of the formulation of that town. The fish is the name of the town. It was a symbol. Our government now gives thanks to celebrate the foundation of that town. It is fascism? No. But it is a means to give another idea about Mussolini. The racial problem, the repression, but he made the town, he made the streets. And so he made also good things. One of the most popular phrases in Italy is yes, Mussolini was bad, but he made… Trains were always on time.

BG: *Did they run on time?*

PS: Trains were always on time.

AC: He didn't do much. Not very good. But he was so capable of communicating what he did.

BG: *Propagandizing.*

PS: Yes. So the people believed.

BG: *Some people say the partisans used* Bella Ciao *in fighting against the fascist regime during World War Two. And others say it was only after World War Two that people began to resurrect that song.*

PS: That song was composed long after the Second World War as a way to glorify the partisan war. But the fact is that Bella Ciao has become the song of the partisans. So the average Italian thinks that that song was sung during the war. And now it's started to have another life, as the song of the antifa.

MR: The Italian right doesn't like *Bella Ciao*. It's a problem, they think it's a left song. For example, when you celebrate the liberation in Italy in some small towns which the right rule, they don't play that song and there was also a verbal fight about it. The problem is the left uses this song as a symbol of the struggle against fascism. And the party of Giorgia Meloni comes from a neo-fascist party. And so they don't like this song.

⌒

After dinner, Antonio promises to send me his two books on the subject, which arrive in my Inbox later in the day. Paolo goes to another room and emerges with my *WAR: The Afterparty* and we sign each other's books, his volume the story of his family's experience during the Mussolini regime.

I book an intentional lengthy layover in Verona for the long train ride to Munich. On arriving, I drag my backpacks out of the station, turn right and walk towards a sign that seems like it's pointing to city center. I start to see signs of city life on both sides of the street and a right turn takes me to a huge plaza with packed outdoor restaurant tables across from a massive arena. The Verona Arena is one of the best-preserved ancient structures of its kind, a Roman amphitheater seating 30,000, built in 30 AD. I don't see many open tables and imagine reservations are needed during peak tourist season on a perfect summer night, so I go to see if I can get a look inside. A staffer near an entrance she shakes her head, *cannot go in, opera tonight, come back tomorrow.*

I am once again soaked in sweat and tuck into a restaurant with fully occupied outdoor tables and a waiter nods and puts me inside in an empty corner by the door. Either because he is nice or because I am quite a sight with bags in tow. I order the branzini with potatoes and a negroni, which is quickly consumed, making room for a second. The website for the opera series says sold out but, after paying my tab, I decide to test the truth of the matter. The ticket saleslady tells me she can place me on the upper level of the arena but no way can I bring in my bags, to the laughter of two older couples. "You should plan in advance," one fellow insists. Thanks, pal. But arena security allows me to stow my bags so I triumphantly return to the ticket desk, head to the top tier of the amphitheater and, though I cannot stay to the end, see a spectacular opera with full orchestra and impressive stage design. The English translation screen is too far to read, so I have no idea what I am watching. Friends the next day ask, what opera did you see? No idea, but I thought I heard a guy calling someone Aida, so that is my story and I'm sticking to it.

NICK CARMODY
Tribalism and Personality Cults

Nick Carmody is a lawyer and psychotherapist and a leading expert and commentator on the psychological and neurological dynamics of cult behaviors in U.S. politics. He is contributor author for the upcoming book, *The MORE Dangerous Case of Donald Trump*. I have followed Nick's social media threads for years for his insights on the unusual connection between Trump and his followers.

I called Nick to ask about the nature of political personality cults.

NC: There's kind of a chameleon effect where they can kind of morph into whatever their followers want. With Trump, being a reality TV star was perfect for him, he was already playing a role. So when he went from having a few people on the production set and playing a role for people to watch on TV, then suddenly got to be in front of thousands of people feeling that energy live, that was intoxicating, to be able to morph into whatever role he wanted in front of them.

This grandiosity and narcissism, they project this larger-than-life persona. It's fake toughness, it's the projection of wealth, the gold toilets. The fact that he was in rap videos, harmless at the time, built up this mythical perception. He's got the supermodel wife. I think the fact that he was fucking porn stars was a benefit to him for a lot of guys, especially in an age where we're dealing with porn addiction. You can say, well, yeah, but he had sex with a porn star without a condom while his wife had a three-month-old, and guys these days are like, where's the part I'm supposed to have a problem with?

For a lot of people—it's generally going to be men—there's an opportunity to live vicariously through him and his grandiosity, his larger-than-life experiences. They're living in a trailer park and they're having trouble getting a date, even having sex, and they feel like they've been chewed up and spit out. Well, here's this guy who's got gold toilets and casinos and he's in rap lyrics and comes across like he's a tough guy. And he's everything that I would love to be. And it's kind of an exchange, he gets to emote through them, right? The grievances, the victimhood, the hate, the anger, the resentment, the vindictiveness, all of that shit.

It's a psy-op; there's a lot of psychological war going on. And for most of us, as a species, we're just not equipped to deal with what's coming at us constantly. I think that that's a huge part of it. Especially when we are so riled up and emotionally reactive and incited constantly.

BG: *You've said there's a tribal element, where if someone is giving you proof about vaccines or election fraud, giving you proof that is impossible, factually, to refute; there is physical pain in your brain or in your body if you know that, by accepting that new information, you will be exiled from your tribe. Which, in the last 300,000 years, would mean you'd be dead, out in the savanna.*

NC: I had used this in a thesis in grad school. And the research showed that areas of the brain that are active when we experience physical pain are also active when we experience social isolation or exclusion. That would suggest that when we do something that causes us to be alienated from a group from which we derive our identity, a sense of community, that there may be something that mimics a physically painful reaction in us. Think about if somebody was to stand up against right now, in a church overwhelmingly pro-Trump and say, 'I know I'm not voting for Trump,' or, 'Hey, I don't believe the election was stolen'. You run the risk of being alienated by your church, by your family, by your friends, your coworkers. So, there's almost a primitive fear of peer pressure, but also the neuro-psychology that creates a strong disincentive to be able to stand up and oppose people in your life with whom you have a sense of community, who you derive your sense of identity from.

> *It's a psy-op, there's a lot of psychological war going on. We're just not equipped to deal with what's coming at us. Especially when we are so riled up and reactive and incited constantly.*

BG: *I watch film of Hitler and Mussolini speaking at rallies. Trump also does rallies. Do you have a sense when you watch those rallies as to what is happening psychologically and biologically?*

NC: You think about any experience humans have where it happens in large groups. If you're at a playoff game for a pro sports team and they score, it's electric, right. You can feel the energy in there. It's not the same if you're at the away team's stadium, and your team scores a touchdown, there's no energy there. If anything, someone's gonna throw a fucking beer at your head. But there's something about being in groups or being in a church and singing hymns or something together, or being at a concert, where everybody in the concert knows the words of a rock song. It's so powerful to be a part of that. And it's even more powerful, when you're a part of something that isn't sports, or music or something like that. And his rallies now very much parallel religious experiences. It almost feels like an Evangelical, music and people raising their hands, like they're being witnesses at Joel Osteen's crushed Blue Velvet carpeting and all that shit. If there was a pain avoidance component to social isolation and exclusion from a group from which you find community identity, then it would make sense that there's probably in the opposite direction, maybe there's oxytocin, right, the neurotransmitter when we hug somebody, when a parent and a child or something like that. Maybe there's a release of oxytocin, there's probably dopamine, there's probably serotonin releases. There's probably a lot of neurochemical experiences going on.

Something else that I think goes with the authoritarian stuff. I wrote an article last year about the hedonic reward of retaliatory aggression in the context of political violence. And in that study what they found was that an area of the brain that was active when we experienced pleasurable experiences was also active when we were engaging in retaliatory aggression. However, that was contingent upon the subject in the study, believing that the other person deserved it. So there had to be the belief that there was a prior provocation. And that's where the victimhood and all of that fear mongering, and that stuff like you know, Tucker Carlson saying, 'They hate you, they hate your children, when they come for you and they will. They've taken your jobs, the immigrants are coming for you, they're contaminating your blood'. All of that shit that makes people scared, and just being scared alone, you feel victimized, right, I don't feel safe in my house, I don't feel safe in my country. You're already a victim without anything having been done to you, just by the experience of not feeling safe.

And so, from that stance, from a subjective point of view, you can create almost anything as a reason for why somebody deserves it. And once that criteria is met, well now we get to a point where I am going to enjoy hurting you. Going back to owning the libs. There was pleasure. I am enjoying basically inflicting a tort action, intentional infliction of emotional distress on my fellow Americans, and watching them get triggered, and I'm enjoying that. And why am I enjoying it? Because they deserve it. Because they're this, or they're that or whatever it is. They're gay, or…

BG: *Traditionally in these authoritarian movements, obviously with Hitler, it's the Jews. It's the Mexicans. It's the Slavs. It's the communists. You look at all these authoritarian leaders, there's this constant hammering and then you get Trump's talking about vermin, people are animals, or that we have to preserve the blood of our country. That stuff is animating people.*

NC: It's easier to hurt someone after you dehumanize them. This is age old. People who are less than human deserve it even more, right? And one of the things that we've seen, you can imagine with the Jews, is all those narratives, the replacement stuff, all the conspiracies around Jews and globalist stuff. You can see why the common citizen, once they believe all that shit, then that satisfies that subjective need, so that the brain can then release dopamine, they can have a pleasurable experience watching Jews getting marched off to Auschwitz, right? These people deserved it. I am enjoying this. That's basically the pleasurable component to sadism. And what happens if we have an experience or engage in a behavior we enjoy, we want to do it more. The more we engage in behavior, the more it becomes habitual, the more it can lean into almost addictive behavior. And from that standpoint, cruelty and inhumanity can mimic addiction, in that context, because you're continuing to engage in behavior that creates a dopamine release. It's just that that behavior is inhumanity and violence or cruelty.

> *It's easier to hurt someone after you dehumanize them. This is age old. People who are less than human deserve it even more, right?*

BG: *On Twitter some years back, you said that the Trump/ Bill Barr/ GOP response to the Black Lives Matter protests highlights the acceleration of the pace of authoritarianism into a full-blown sprint.*

NC: I remembered that thread. I think that was when he was at Lafayette Square, where (Joints Chiefs Chairman Mark) Milley went out there with them, a photo op for him to go out there and hold up the Bible in front of that church after they cleared the square. Later in the thread, authoritarianism is defined as the enforcement of strict obedience to authority at the expense of personal freedom. Although the right fetishize this freedom, the reality is that they've sold their soul for Trump and judges that they hoped would deny other people freedom and rights. And furthermore, fascism is defined as far right ultra-national authoritarianism that is characterized by dictatorial power, forcible suppression of opposition, and strong regimentation of society and the economy. Obviously, we've seen a lot of that lately with Dobbs. And, for all their talk about freedom, they definitely have a penchant to want to control citizens. It's basically, we want freedom to do whatever the hell we want, but we want to control the things that we disagree with.

I wrote something a few years back about an Eric Metaxas and Franklin Graham video, where they were saying that opposing Trump was demonic. And my response to that was, opposing a sociopathic narcissist isn't demonic. It's democratic. It's what we do in this country. And I think that obviously, anytime you're using the word evil or demonic, those are dog whistles for the evangelicals because they see the world in very binary terms. It's very us and them. It's believers and non-believers and anybody who is against them. When Trump is the chosen one, the leader handpicked by God, it's really easy for them to frame that in a very binary evil/ good, demonic/ holy frame of mind, and it gets a lot of traction. One of the problems with that is that we are such a polarized government, it becomes really hard to get anything done in a democratic country with the premise, or at least the foundation, that it is about compromise. Because you can't ever compromise with the quote, unquote enemy if they are evil, if they are demonic. Because otherwise you're complicit. Now you are complicit with evil and demonism and it just basically paralyzes any functioning government. In that same thread, I wrote, when people who have been conditioned to accept and embrace an authoritarian belief system enter the political arena, it is inevitable that they will eventually weaponize their faith and their followers to create a political structure that mirrors their religious authoritarianism. This is why it's extremely dangerous to have religion intertwined with politics, because expecting the Christian right to accept that dissenting political point of view is equivalent to expecting them to accept the coexistence of beliefs in a non-Christian God or the absence of a God. That's where we're headed.

Trump feels like the luckiest motherfucker I've ever observed. And that's such a stark contrast, if something happened to Biden, there would be a huge wave of momentum, to have somebody younger on the Democratic ticket, and all of the media coverage and everything that would be going on with that, that could, especially if it's a black woman. But, yeah as of right now, today, it feels like a fucking out of control freight train.

CHAPTER 5

GERMANY

Hitler Was Elected

Whereupon I meet with Hermann Göring's great niece… a walkabout past Munich's historical Nazi landmarks… a Friday night train to Tutsing for a lakeside Bavarian dinner with Veronika… a walk through the Nazi Documentation Centre with Markos… a train ride to the Dachau Concentration Camp… a chat with German political thinkers Patrick and Ingar.

The train out of Verona is late. Scheduled for 11pm, the departure time is now uncertain. There are no shops open in the station. I wander the hallways out of boredom and exhaustion, hoping to stumble onto a café. It is unclear where the restrooms might be. Back on the platform, voila, a vending machine. It's not advised to be eating snacks before sleeping but any manner of stimulation seems urgent. My comrades for this unexpected and unwelcome platform congregation include a hearty mix of young backpackers, elders, anxious solo travelers. Alas, the train arrives half past midnight and an older gentleman herds people in, explaining how to get to numbered berths. One young woman behind me bearing a massive backpack demands she gets an entire compartment to herself. The beleaguered train attendant, having heard it all before, insists, no, she gets to share it with five strangers. My own sleeper accommodation is ridiculously tight but I take a sleeping pill and vanish into oblivion. We get into München Hauptbahnhof, Munich Central Station, just past sunrise. I taxi to my destination and, once again, the hotelier cheerfully allows me an 8am check in. The hotel is a short walk to a neighborhood train station and around the corner from Theresienwiese, ground zero for Oktoberfest. I promise myself a proper German meal there on my way out of town.

Bettina Sellers is the grandniece of senior Nazi official Hermann Göring. A mutual friend introduces us. Göring was a World War One fighter pilot and the last commander serving under Baron von Richthofen, widely known as the Red Baron. He was among those wounded in Hitler's failed Beer Hall Putsch in 1923. While receiving treatment, he developed an addiction to morphine that lasted until his trial as a war criminal in Nuremberg. Designated as heir apparent to Adolf Hitler, he was commander-in-chief of the Luftwaffe (German air force). One of his early acts as cabinet minister was to supervise the creation of the Gestapo, the Nazi secret police. After exploring the Göring family history through her adult life, Sellers recently published a book, *The Good Uncle*, providing a unique inside look into the psychology and social behavior of Nazi officials responsible for the mass murder of ethnic, political, and national groups deemed unworthy of living by the party. We meet in her living room with her husband, Adi Pieper.

BETTINA SELLERS
The Good Uncle

BG: *Why write the book?*

BS: Why? It's a healing process for me, to come to terms with it. It's a very hard thing. When you really look at what these guys did, and my grandmother was also rather involved.

BG: *In what way?*

BS: She was one of the head positions in the Red Cross. Thanks to Hermann. She was very close to him, and he did a lot of (nepotism). My grandfather, her husband, he died just when the whole thing started in 1932, of injuries from the First World War. And so he sort of took care of her father a little bit, and she had three boys, aged 8 or 10 to 12. My father was the oldest and he got them into the Napola. It's the top Nazi boarding school. And then two of them became fighter pilots. My father had eye problems, so he only became later a pilot, when they needed some more reconnaissance.

BG: *In watching your interview at the Santa Fe Film Festival , there was a Red Cross facility that became a sort of waystation for people who would then be sent on to the concentration camp.*

BS: Can you believe it, my grandmother who was in that position stated later on in life, this all didn't happen. I mean, she must have been right there.

BG: *Someone said to me recently, people who wanted to believe what happened knew what happened. People who didn't want to know what happened or didn't want to believe it, completely denied it.*

BS: I know. While we were in Germany, we saw *The Zone of Interest*. Did you see that?

BG: *Yes, of course.*

BS: Oh, my God. Very well done. I mean, there were just right next to it and kind of pretended all life was good. That's what happened.

BG: *You describe your great uncle in many ways as a caring and charming fellow.*

BS: To his family, yeah.

BG: *While he was responsible for enormous human suffering. You're a student of Eastern philosophy and spiritual practice. What have you concluded about the human condition? Where educated, thoughtful men, like your great uncle can exhibit such kindness in their personal lives and such great horror in their public lives?*

BS: I think that's a big question about humankind. There can be both good and evil in one person. I mean, obviously, a lot of these guys must have been psychopaths to do so much evil. However, apparently, part of them was still able to feel kindness. You see this with mafia guys.

BG: *They love their family. That's the whole thing about* The Godfather *and* The Sopranos, *you know, they're family men.*

BS: And so it's possible. I don't know about Hitler.

BG: *In the Riefenstahl movies, he loves puppies and little children.*

BS: Exactly. He had a dog all the time. He was very charming. In the end, he was going more and more mad. But when he was at the big rallies, he would shake hands, he was extremely personable and nice and generous and whatnot. If you give people that much power and there is no end to it, they will use it and do the most horrible things, whether it's Mao Zedong, or some of the guys now, Kim Jong Un, or Hitler or the other Nazis. I think that is the problem. If there are no consequences to their actions, they will do the most horrible things.

Look at Trump. God. I think the most dangerous thing right now is if Trump gets elected. I will do whatever I can to stop that. But this is a prime example of how somebody goes nuts with too much power and too much adoration and all the people around him applaud him, no matter what he does, no matter what nonsense he does, it's unbelievable. And it was probably similar around Hitler. And he seems to be even a bit more intelligent than Trump.

> *I think that is the problem. If there are no consequences to their actions, they will do the most horrible things.*

BG: *Mussolini was a journalist, he wrote books, was thoughtful, was a pro-labor social justice advocate for a long while.*

BS: Intelligence doesn't mean people have to be kind, rather the opposite. The Nazis were a bit different, in that they were a bit revolutionary, because they were all fairly young compared to other regimes before. Like all the Weimar Republic, they were all old guys. 70s, 80s. And before that was the Kaiser, also very old. Himmler and some of these guys were in their 30s or 40s when it started. And not all of them were highly educated. But that was the appeal for them, to have something new, to serve something revolutionary. Hermann, my great uncle was from the upper class compared to some of these other guys. That's why Hitler used him for certain things.

BG: Do you think, is there a natural inclination among humans to seek strongmen like Adolf Hitler?

BS: We were just talking about that this morning because this is going on, as people are so insecure, they want to have some strong leader. I hope it changes a bit, but it's happening again right now, no?

I mean, the whole world was really at wits end after the First World War. Also not to forget, not only the 20 million people died, but they had also the flu epidemic where another 20 million people died. And it was pretty horrible, in Germany they had an unbelievable collapse of the economy, Wall Street broke down in the U.S., all that stuff. People were very insecure. So they wanted somebody to fix that.

BG: What attracted him (Göring) to Hitler?

BS: It was the beer putsch, the first time he walked into the campaign thing, the party had just started. He was taken by Hitler. Totally. Why? You tell me. I don't know. Maybe also he looked for a strongman. He was pretty strong himself. I mean, like leader material. But he loved him.

BG: Do you think anytime from then until the end of World War Two until his death that he had regrets?

BS: If he did, he didn't mention those in the Nuremberg trials. He didn't apologize or do any such thing. I mean the way he dealt with it; he was full of drugs. A lot of them were. He was on morphine a lot because he had pain. And they weaned him off when he was in prison with the Americans. That's when he also lost all the weight.

BG: Hitler at one point announced in the late 30s that Goering would be his successor. And then when Hitler was about to commit suicide, he called in that card, Hitler was enraged and….

BS: He was enraged about everybody. The same about Himmler. He thought Himmler was following him. And he was enraged about him when he took charge. He was just such a maniac.

BG: *Even at that point, do you think he thought there's something a little odd about this Hitler fellow?*

BS: Unbelievable. I mean, what delusions did he have? Then he went to the Americans and thought he would get away with it all.

BG: *Probably better than going to the Soviets.*

BS: Yeah, for sure. That was smart of him. The Soviets would have killed him right away. Or maybe they would have also done a big tribunal. I don't know. Unbelievable.

BG: *Why do you think many Germans today still think fondly of Hitler?*

BS: I don't know who really does think fondly of Hitler. They must be pretty old. Or they know nothing about what happened.

BG: *But there is a neo-Nazi movement and a far-right movement of people who think that Hitler was a pretty swell fellow.*

BS: Yeah. But there's like five, six percent. They didn't even get into the parliament. And then they were forbidden for a while. They was for the most time pretty small. What's happening now, they have a new thing, it's called AfD. And they are, especially in the East, really big. Some places they have 20 percent, which is really scary.

BG: *And what is the appeal of those followers of that party?*

BS: I think it's the same story. They are insecure, they want a strong leader. What Hitler did way back then, he made the Jewish people to be responsible for everything. Now it's the foreign people. The Ausländer.

BG: *You've lived in the United States. Do you see any parallels between 1930s Germany and present-day America?*

BS: Yes and no. If we remember the 1930s in America, there was a time of the Depression, people really didn't have enough to eat. And in Germany, it was after losing the First World War. The people are not doing so badly right now. I mean, they're not hungry, and they have even health insurance and this and that and social security. In spite of that, there is a lot of fear about the future. And for good reason, because the environment is changing very rapidly, whether people want to admit that or not. The right generally thrives on fear of God knows what, whether it's the foreign people coming in or it's people trying to get you.

And so the reality is people are not doing so badly and still the fear is there. And it's being fanned bigly from Mister Bigly, Mister Trump. But all the rightist guys, they all have that same agenda. And I find it really worrisome because we lived a long time in America and it seemed to be a democracy at work, even though people argued all the time, and there was the right and the left, but they seemed to be working together in Congress. People respected each other. That has gone out the window, and the people who want Trump and the Republican Party, this MAGA right, they want no limits. And the 'No Limits' is what happened then in the Nazi time, and that is deadly. God knows what they want to do with that. And America is a country of immigrants. Trump's family were immigrants. Everybody of this MAGA people were immigrants. We were immigrants. The only natives were the Native Americans, and they probably came from somewhere at some point.

BG: *What do you think Americans can expect if Trump were reelected?*

BS: An end to the rule of law. That's what I'm afraid of. That they want to rule without consequences. Yeah. And that they have all the people in the judiciary, they already tried this. I mean, they already have a majority in the Supreme Court. And there are some people who are not exactly following the rule of law. That's the problem. If you have people who can be somewhere for life. What a stupid idea, the Supreme Court, there's no consequences when they behave badly. Not a good idea. So anyways, that is their strategy. They've been putting as many judges as possible in and then they blocked others, this has been going on for quite some time. They blocked all the Democratic nominations. We've been following all that. We still do. And it's very dangerous. They might not have an agenda to invade other countries like Hitler did in the end but who knows what they come up with.

> *It seems people respected each other. That has gone out the window, and this MAGA right, they want no limits. And the 'No Limits' is what happened then in the Nazi time, and that is deadly.*

A Short History of Adolf Hitler's Rise to Power

1918-1919: Germany loses World War I. The Treaty of Versailles imposes harsh reparations, causing widespread economic hardship and political instability. The punitive reparations of the Treaty of Versailles breed extreme nationalist sentiments.

1919-1923: The Weimar Republic is established, a period marked by economic crisis, hyperinflation, and political extremism.

1923: The Beer Hall Putsch. Hitler's failed coup attempt in Munich leads to his imprisonment, where he writes *Mein Kampf*. Hitler's trial and imprisonment transform him into a national figure.

1924-1929: The Nazi Party, still a fringe group, gains traction during economic recovery, skillfully exploiting every crisis, tapping into a reservoir of discontent.

1929: The Great Depression begins, severely affecting Germany, leading to massive unemployment.

1930: Nazis gain a significant number of seats in the Reichstag (the German parliament).

1932: Hitler runs for president, but loses to Paul von Hindenburg (president of the Weimar Republic from 1925 to his death in 1934); however, the Nazi Party becomes the largest in the Reichstag.

1933: Hitler is appointed Chancellor. The Reichstag Fire leads to the Reichstag Fire Decree, curtailing civil liberties, crushing political opposition, and establishing a de facto dictatorship.

1934: Night of the Long Knives. Hitler purges the government and party and consolidates power.

1935: The Nuremberg Laws are enacted, institutionalizing racial discrimination.

MARKUS NAEGELE
A Walk Through NS-Dokumentationszentrum, Munich

The Munich Documentation Center for the History of National Socialism presents the history of Nazism on the site of the former 'Brown House', headquarters of the National Socialist German Workers Party (NSDAP). Between 1933 and 1945, the area around Munich's Königsplatz became the Nazi regime's central administrative area. I locate the key buildings of the Reich on a map and visit as many as I can during my stay.

The museum opened in 2015. Each floor represents an era in the gradual dismantling of Germany's democratic institutions as the Nazis come to power. From a seemingly clumsy extremist group with a cartoonish, histrionic leader in Adolf Hitler, year by year, the party grows in influence and effectiveness and, once in power, unleashes fascism's most bitter end game and a war that takes more than 70 million lives. Brown House is ground zero for the affliction that would infect the country and the continent and Markus Naegele is a skilled partner for the walk through the Center.

Born in Cologne in the mid-sixties, Naegele spent years in the music business as a journalist, musician, concert booker, radio DJ, and band manager. He moved to Munich in 1998 to become a book editor for Heyne Verlag and, in 2005, founded Heyne Hardcore as publishing director, a boutique imprint of Penguin Random House Germany for 'cultish fiction and nonfiction books'. As a singer and songwriter, he recorded four albums with his bands *Fuck Yeah* and *Don Marco & Die Kleine Freiheit*. He lives in Munich with his wife and four cats.

I thought I had a straight shot to the meeting place, punctuality being an important asset in a project like this. But there is some kind of massive summer music festival with long lines and I have to walk all the way round the neighborhood. Upon arrival, the building is nondescript without immediately evident signage, and the security in front don't know the name of the building they are securing. So I walk round the block again then, finally, there is Markus, hard to miss in his red t-shirt. We greet each other and start our tour on the floor showcasing the aftermath of Germany's defeat in World War One.

BG: *After World War One—in Italy as well—you have a lot of men with guns.*

MS: The *Freikorps*, the freedom fighters, they were just battling each other. (Freikorps *were German and other European paramilitary units that fought as mercenaries from the 18th through the early 20th centuries.*) They have some great material here, so that's a lot of stuff to read. When you see this (*pointing to photos of street conflicts alongside long text descriptions in German and English*), the new political left was divided. It's just what's happening today. All the left parties are so divided. It's part of the problem. So everyone was battling each other.

We walk to the other end of the exhibit floor, past well-curated glass covered displays with carefully selected news articles, flyers, captions, and memorabilia. I'm worried that I cannot absorb it all. We stop a friendly museum staffer and, complimenting her team on a marvelous facility, ask if all this might be available online. No, she replies, apologetically, with a smile. But I can buy a catalog, also available in English. We go by the bookstore and it is a massive volume. I can't carry any more books in my already overstuffed bags. Markus kindly offers to mail one to me and buys one for himself. We pass by some Nazi propaganda displays.

MN: At the moment in Germany, the problem is that the far right are very active on TikTok, they somehow get the young people. That's the thing that is really frustrating, because you always thought the young people, the next generation will be clever enough, will be educated enough. And now other parties try to get on social media, to follow up, but it's difficult for them.

BG: *How would you characterize the young male who's feeling the lack of a future, who may be feeling that starting a family is out of reach, has heard that catastrophic climate events may be in his future. There is immigration from the Middle East, you have a million displaced people from Ukraine. So that young guy on Tik Tok who is not aligned with progressive green views, what is that person thinking as all that propaganda is coming at him?*

MN: I always thought that people are smart enough and educated enough to not follow these simple solutions.

BG: *But you'd be wrong.*

MN: Because there are no simple solutions. Germany has been a pretty wealthy country after the 50s. And I think people want to stick to their wealth. They want to go three times a year on holiday. And if they can only do it twice, they will elect a different government.

They don't have any solutions. They just attack the whole time. At the moment, I was glad that there is a new government. There were there was high hopes in the beginning, like the first month, everyone was like, this is going to be great. The Socialist party, the Greens, and the Federal party, and then they have to react to one crisis after another and they can't really make their own politics. So they are easily attacked because there are no simple solutions. And then if you look at the news, and if you see at the moment what Trump is saying, it's all simple solutions. It's all, it's going to be great. I'm going to...

BG: *And only I... isn't that a Hitlerian kind of a statement? When Trump says, only I can solve this problem?*

MN: It's kind of the idea of this museum. There's a risk that history repeats itself. And I was taught, especially in Germany, after two wars, I always thought there will never be a strong right-wing party again. I was very, very sure about that, there will always be a percentage of right-wing people with their minds, but it'll be like five or 10 percent maximum. And now we're talking about maybe 20 percent. In the east of Germany, it's close to 30 percent.

I always thought that the AfD was simply a protest party, but it's become more now. And that's the problem. And look at France. But I always thought that Germans are smart enough. They should be smart enough with the history.

BG: *They should have been smart enough in 1935 also. It was one of the most advanced cultures in the world, German philosophy and medicine and architecture and science, music, arts…*

MN: I believe in simple things like peace, love and understanding. Everything that fascism gave us, cold people, hate. You don't have to be too smart to understand and see where things are going.

(Vice Presidential Republican candidate J.D.) Vance does smart speeches, and even in Germany, his book was considered a really interesting look at why Trump got elected. And if you see what he said, a couple years ago.

BG: *He said Trump was like a Hitler.*

MN: And now he's promoting him. And people have no second thoughts.

And then Trump's got his ear in a huge bandage (the assassination attempt was days before). And he's got the camera, he's standing, you can always see his ear. So people have their ear masks. And he's got these big screens where you see him being shot. And then he does his big speeches about unity. It's like a huge Hollywood spectacle. And people somehow, I think it's like parody, it's like the worst. But people love it. They cheer. And they go crazy.

But it didn't come from one day to another. Even in the 20s, Hitler tried to make a point and he tried to assemble people, he got people in prison, people made fun of him, he tried to get his party going, he was a total disaster. But then, through some circumstances, he gained power. And very quickly then. And that's the thing that concerns me. For many years in the U.S., as well as in Germany, you had the conservative party, you had the socialist party, and it was always a little bit up and down. But now you've got these huge waves and you see this in all of Europe, you've got this back and forth. Nowadays media is always about disaster after disaster.

> *But it didn't come from one day to another. Even in the 20s, Hitler tried to make a point and people made fun of him; he was a total disaster. But then, through some circumstances, he gained power.*

The NSDAP, in the early 20s tried to gain access to Munich high society and get money to build the party. And then in 1925 Hitler was officially banned from public speaking in Bavaria. So that's eight years before he finally gained power.

He was taken to prison in 1924 for five years. During his time in prison, he wrote the first part of *Mein Kampf*. He was supposed to be five years in prison and got released after nine months. In 1923 when he tried to do his putsch, it was during the big crisis of the Weimar Republic, after the first World War, there were the reparation payments, Deutsche Marks inflation. There was a lot of unemployment. *(From a value of 4.2 per dollar on the eve of World War I, the mark depreciated to 4.2 trillion per dollar by November 1923.)*

At the same time you had Mussolini in Italy, October 22 starting his movement. If you look at the European Union at the moment, the right-wing parties try to get together, to try to make a bond. This is kind of the same thing you had with Mussolini and Hitler.

BG: *With Hitler increasingly blaming it on the Jews.*

MN: When Hitler did his speeches or demonstrations, it was always a big spectacle. It's the same thing with Trump, when I watch these rallies or whatever he does, it's all the cheering, all the stomping, all the repeating of slogans. Now if you have Trump, you have the *'fight, fight'* pose. It's almost like *heil, heil,* it's not much different. It's very simple. One word. And again, it's the simple solutions people go for.

I think a lot of people are bored of politics, think politics is not for me. They want entertainment, so Trump gives them entertainment, they want emotions, he gives them emotions. Whenever Trump appears there's something to talk about, good or bad. And somehow people are affected by it. A lot of politicians just do their job, and I think politicians should do their job, which is to do politics. But it doesn't seem to be the state of the art at the moment. And whatever he does it's always big cinema.

If you look at these Nazi rallies, look into the faces of people, it's the same kind of aggression. Same kind of total conviction thing.

BG: *Is that a key part of it? We are victims, and we have grievances, and those people are responsible for it.*

MN: But he falls on open ears because there's a lot of competition in society at the moment about wealth. Basically, I want more than the other. He has a bigger house; I want the bigger house than the neighbor. And that's part of the world crisis we have. The economic crisis. If you have competition, you want to fight the other, you want to be more successful than the other.

> *If you look at these rallies, look into the faces*
> *of people, it's the same kind of aggression.*
> *Same kind of total conviction thing.*

BG: *It's a lot easier to say your problem is because of immigrants than to say your problem is because since Ronald Reagan there's been no increase in your average earning power.*

MN: But it's too difficult for a lot of people. It's easier to say, if we get rid of these few then we'll be healthier. And we'll have three more beers every night to drink.

So they came into power in January 1933. Already, in the beginning, they took 5,000 political enemies and put them in prison within a very, very quick time.

They built a concentration camp right after coming into power. (*Dachau, a half hour outside Munich by train, was built in March 1933*).

Here you've got the end of democracy in Munich, and again very, very quickly, they had a ban on all other parties in July, like six months after they gained power.

BG: *It struck me in the beginning of the exhibition, in 1919, there were socialists or anarchists saying that parliamentary democracy will not deliver the Germany that we need, they wanted a Soviet model. Democracy doesn't work.*

MN: Democracy is always a hard battle. Basically, no one wants to do compromises. I'm not good at doing compromises when I do my artistic work. But in the end, it is the only way to live together. It's part of the deal.

BG: *Hitler around this time, was he thinking, how can we do the best for the average German to bring them prosperity and peace coming out of the ashes of World War One or is he obsessed with gaining* *power, retribution against enemies, and killing the people he hated, like the Jews?*

MN: He wanted the big Reich, he wanted to be the leader of the super Reich. I don't think he had in mind the small worker's prosperity. I think it was about him being in charge of the whole machine, and maybe the whole world, and being immortal. I think he was crazy. But the plans are all laid out for the 1,000-year Reich.

BG: *In the United States when I was a kid, 30-40 percent of the working population was unionized. Now, it's 10 percent and the right wing is just constantly hammering away at organized labor.*

MN: Because as a dictator, you don't want anyone speaking up against you, for sure.

That's the same thing as today. If you look at the problem of the AfD, the Alternative for Germany, which is weird enough as a name, they have a lot of voters from the working class or poor, but the politics, if you look at their programs. It's not as if the simple man will gain anything. It was the same with Hitler. So it's kind of a paradox, that people vote for them. The same I think in the U.S., when American workers, or black or a lot of women voted for Trump. He should be the enemy, so why are they doing that? I have no idea why they did that. It's paradox. Sometimes politics are weird.

—

There's a growing sense of dread as we approach the exhibits of the late 30s and World War Two. This well-curated building slowly reveals disturbing and prescient signs of what's to come. At each step, it's normalized and behaviors previously unthinkable are everyday occurrences. Internationally, Chamberlain and Daladier try to make peace with the Nazi regime—understandable after the trench warfare horrors of World War One—but are duped in the September 1938 Munich Agreement as Hitler occupies the Czechoslovakia and enters Prague in March 1939, with the world war starting later that year.

The first floors of the museum keep the experience in the head, historical facts, artifacts, political analysis. The rise of the Hitler movement in Munich. The failed Hitler coup in 1923. The commutation of his prison sentence for treason as the prevailing government failed to understand the danger of a future, more successful attempt to seize the reins of power. In Landsberg Prison, Hitler dictates Nazi manifesto *Mein Kampf* to fellow inmates Emil Maurice and Rudolf Hess. As an American, the cinematic Nazi villains were monstrous, far removed, unfamiliar. *We're not like those people.* This could never happen here. But these exhibits from WWI, the 20s, the 30s, all look familiar to me. The raging over ethnic minorities. The escalating aggression. The militias manipulated by the Nazi leadership, beating people in the streets. The Proud Boys leading the violent assault on the U.S. Capitol on January 6, 2021, in an attempt to block the peaceful transfer of power, egged on by Trump, who refused to intercede. The Republican National Committee called the attack, which wounded more than one hundred police officers and trashed the Capitol, 'legitimate political discourse'.

The Nazi leaders are well-dressed, civilized, Hitler in a country suit and fedora, lounging on the grass next to his German shepherd, speaking in terms that veiled his barbarism. Hitler rose to the top, as did Trump, by knowing how to sound sane enough for the Lutheran shopkeeper in Munich to listen, agree, and, finally, vote him into power. From an underestimated fringe party, the outrages became normalized, the fevered racism accepted. Year by year by year, the NSDAP (Nazi) party grew in electoral popularity until they gained power, democratically, in 1933. And, to paraphrase Donald Trump, if you voted for them in that election, you would have no need to vote in the years ahead.

There's a map of the Nazi party offices. I walked past many of them on the way here, touching the buildings, looking through windows, imagining the mundane daily trappings of party governance, first filling out forms, then planning the mass murder of Jews, Poles, Russians, Roma, dissidents, journalists.

From 1921, Hitler declared Munich would always be the headquarters of the movement. The 'Brown House', location of this center, was the heart of power on the *Königsplatz*. The offices in the district would spread across 68 buildings populated by 6,000 employees. The architecture of the Centre by Berlin architect Georg Scheel Wetzel was designed to signal a fundamental break with the location's history and neighborhood.

> *"The compulsion of this regime to glorify itself with pompous and grand architecture that is as megalomaniac as it is artistically impoverished is a passion with a strongly pathological streak."* —THOMAS MANN, 1938

We continue our walk through exhibition areas. The gradual end of the rule of law and democratic norms. The public humiliation of lawyer Michael Siegel, a well-respected Munich Jew. Heroic stories of students, journalists, activists who at each step pushed back against the rising tide of Nazism, with more vicious and deadly consequences as each year passed. The photo essays humanize the resistance, the risks taken, the refusal to be indifferent to injustice. They move the experience from the head to the heart. Underground printing presses. Posters and flyers. The preeminent role of members of the labor organizations. The haranguing of anyone in opposition as communists, *der Bolschevismus*. The normality of it all, the middle-aged good Germans on their bicycles giving the Nazi salutes as they ride by. The refusal of Lutheran and other churches to publicly criticize Nazi crimes. Markos continues:

MN: When Hitler took over, the unemployment rate began to drop, because everyone was working on the big plan. It was the start of the Autobahn. So, it was kind of a big success, in terms of labor. But all for his dream. And he took steps really quickly. Some people liked that, at least he's taking action. I think Trump could be the same thing.

BG: *Although in his four years he was a failure in everything from funding infrastructure to responding to a pandemic.*

MN: I think he had a phone call with Zelensky, telling him, I will end the war quickly. People think yeah cool. Great. But under what conditions people don't ask.

These are photos of the Hitler youth. My father was also in the Hitler youth. Anyone 10 to 18 years, boys and girls, more or less had to go to Hitler youth. If you didn't, you were like an outsider.

BG: *How deep seated was antisemitism in Germany before Hitler became popular?*

MN: There's always been antisemitism in Germany, for sure. I think he needed a scapegoat. And they (Jews) were in the economy, they were in the higher ranks. So they were maybe an easy, bigger target.

In April 1933, three months after they came to power, they already had an anti-Jewish boycott. But it wasn't just the Jews, it was also the Sinti and the Roma. They also stigmatized all the homosexuals and basically everyone that didn't look German.

My father, who's 95 now, he was born in 1928, he doesn't really like to talk a lot about the time. They wanted to have him into the war. So his parents hid him away somewhere in Bavaria for a while. But when I asked him how it happened, he will say, well, we didn't really know. And I think it's impossible. This is impossible. Even today, some of my friends are very cynical about politics, a lot of the more liberal people. And they are passive, even the last American elections, when it was a close race between Biden and Trump, people all said, it doesn't really matter. And I was like, what?

—

I head down to Tutsing on the comfortable and reliable S-Bahn for a lakeside Bavarian dinner with my friend Veronika. After a walk down the Brahms Promenade, enjoying a view of the Starnberger See and the nearby Alps, I order an imposing bayerische Schweinshaxe along with a beer and other local treats. Veronika asks for half portions but the counter fellow doesn't listen and I will be digesting this meal for days. After getting back to Munich, I walk past the train station's trestle. Couples and teens and friends climb up and watch the trains come and go. Others were here when I left at sunset and this new group of dangling legs dots the nighttime view. I take a leisurely walk back to my hotel. Tomorrow, I visit Dachau.

INGAR SOLTY

Maintaining the Facade

Ingar Solty is a German political writer with a Ph.D. from York University in Toronto, Canada. A Senior Research Fellow in Foreign, Peace and Security Policy at the Rosa Luxemburg Foundation's Institute for Critical Social Analysis in Berlin, he founded the North Atlantic Left Dialogue, an annual summit of left-wing intellectuals. He is also the social movements and politics editor in the German periodical *Das Argument*. He has numerous published articles on fascism, Marxism, and far-right populism.

IS: Fascism is a historical term. That means it always adapts to the historic moments. And therefore, the shape it takes differs over time. I think that fascism historically, obviously, was connected to nationalist politics and imperialist politics, a cult of violence, a cult of masculinity. And that changed quite dramatically over time, connected to the development of historic capitalism. I think that it is a useful differentiation to distinguish between fascist movements and fascism as a state of rule, or as a system. And so, in the contemporary day and age, it's possible to have fascist movements that don't necessarily implement a fascist state. They don't necessarily eliminate liberal parliamentarianism, universal suffrage, etc.

BG: *Why is a cult of masculinity central to fascist movements or, more broadly, to far right or quasi-conservative movements today?*

IS: David Horowitz said something along the lines that the right knows not what it's for, but what it's against. And so unlike liberalism and socialism which have a coherent vision of how to order society, how to order the economy, the right never had that. Therefore, as a result, we have a market-oriented conservatism, but we also have a historical anti-capitalist conservatism, which was largely connected to the land-owning classes. And we still today have so called economic conservatives, social conservatives, but it means something different in the American diction. There were conservatives that tried to be social reformers, very statist. We still have that kind of currency, even though it's very weak today. And so I think that the right knows what it's against, it's reactionary in the strict sense, it reacts to historic moments. I would say that it lacks a coherent theory of economy and society. It only responds to the symptoms of global capitalism, as opposed to the root causes. For instance, it will be against crime, but not against economic inequality, or social inequality as the root cause of crime. It is against migrants, but it's not against free trade, which has caused the displacement of people, a proletarianization of hundreds of millions of people in the Global South. And the same applies to gender relations.

> *Fascism, historically, was connected to
> nationalist politics and imperialist politics,
> a cult of violence, a cult of masculinity.*

BG: *You're an observer of global politics. As someone who's studied closely your own country's embrace of fascism, what concerns might you have about an American fascist future?*

IS: When Trump won in 2016, he was an iconic figure of the far right. Just as Milei in Argentina is now. I think Nicos Poulantzas, the Greek-French theorist, was right in his analysis of historic fascism. That fascism comes to power when the situation has become so untenable and unendurable for large segments of the popular classes, and the left does not offer a vision that is inclusionary, a path out of the status quo which has become untenable, that the far-right parties fill the vacuum. It wasn't a coincidence that in 2015, this whole idea of a social egalitarian, democratic Europe was defeated in the Eurozone crisis in Greece. Then right afterwards, you had the migrant crisis and following from that the rise of the far right. You can see it, essentially the right-wing parties made much more gains since 2015 and 2016, which is also when Trump came into power. That was a boost for the far right obviously. You had Brexit then, also under right wing terms. And so obviously a victory for Trump in the U.S. will also substantially help the far right in Europe.

> *Fascism comes to power when the situation has
> become so untenable and unendurable for large
> segments of the popular classes, and the left does not
> offer a path out of the status quo which has become
> untenable, that the far-right parties fill the vacuum.*

BG: *Do you think there's always been a fascist streak in U.S. politics?*

IS: Starting with Huey Long, or like a lot of the 30s politics, Richard Hofstetter analyzed in his paranoid style that there always was that movement. Like I said, I think it's important to distinguish between the movement and a fascist state.

The term fascism is often used as a vehicle to mobilize the democratic base, to say that the barbarians are at the gate. And then extreme right politicians like Trump do not abolish universal suffrage or the liberal parliamentarian system. But I think also that it's important to note that the historic far right acted under the memory of constitutional or non-constitutional monarchism. And that the historic right in the 19th century wants to go back to that. And that people, like the most visionary or intelligent extreme right thinkers like Carl Schmitt (prominent Nazi political thinker) noted that they would have to, if they wanted to eliminate liberal parliamentarianism, find a new base for it, which was essentially fascism.

The far right, those forces which would have been fascists in the 1920s and 30s, underwent learning processes. What was obvious was that historic fascism was responsible for World War Two and the Holocaust, etc. But the right-wing libertarians and fascists were facing the same problem, how to essentially limit mass democracy. (Austrian economist Friedrich von) Hayek was just much better at solving that problem. You could maintain the facade, people could still vote, but he would essentially remove large sectors of the actual decisions or the important decisions on the economy, on financial politics, etc., from the electorate. So people would still have the feeling that they're voting or that the decision matters. But in essence, liberalism has become post-democratic. We find in the far right, in the AfD for instance in Germany, they buy into the Murray Rothbard ideology, like let's limit the right to vote to those who pay into the system, who are not beneficiaries of transfer payments to the welfare state. So the unemployed and the pensioners, the retired people should not be allowed to vote. We do have those arguments still in the far right.

PATRICK VATER
Advertising, Propaganda, and the Decline of Political Education

PV: I was born in the south, in Mannheim. I moved to Hamburg for a couple of years when I was young, then I lived in London for a couple of years where I did a degree in Communications Studies and Cultural Studies. And then I came to Berlin in 1999 and started working in advertising. And at the same time, I've always been a musician. So I've been touring, I've been releasing music for many years, and my project or my baby is this band called Rodeo FM, it's a country band. And we're doing left wing country, which itself is a bit of its own genre, because country music isn't always very progressive. We have this slightly communist, Marxist angle. And I think that's a bit of a novelty.

BG: *A Nashville country music critic once calculated that more than half the most popular songs one year included some combination of a pickup truck, a dog, a shotgun, a Confederate flag, and a young woman in skinny jeans.*

PV: Yeah, actually I think this is already getting to the core of what your project is about. I see two different streams where progressive and reactionary tendencies play out. And one is the whole identity thing, which is about diversity and how people frame themselves, gay rights, and racism and all that. There's of course progressive elements in that. But it's at the same time very 'new liberal', just to keep it at that. And there's this other axis, which is about distribution of wealth. And that has been totally hijacked by the right, by Donald Trump, in Germany and Europe as well. The right says, okay, capitalism is about exploiting the poor and, of course it's right in the analysis, it's not right in the way they would go about it. But these two axes, this identity/ minorities thing, and the distribution thing, they are sort of played against each other. And the left has abandoned that distribution thing because they're all part of the system. And that is the problem, why the right is getting so strong. And that circles back to the rednecks, because a lot of them are disenfranchised. There is no platform for them. Guys like Bernie Sanders, or whoever you might have in Europe, they're just too classical liberal, and the rednecks, the disenfranchised, can't identify with that. So who's left? It's like the hijackers. It's like guys like Donald Trump, or the AfD in Germany.

BG: *As a remote German observer watching American culture, doesn't it strike you as bizarre that Trump followers see this billionaire born with a silver spoon in his mouth, who shits on a golden toilet, who takes photos in gilded surroundings, who any New Yorker can tell you has a history of stiffing working people, stiffing contractors… this guy is the hero of the working class?*

PV: Of course, he's a total liar. But people don't care about that. They're just so fed up with the system. Rightly so. You know, at the end of the day, I don't see much difference between the politics of the Democrats and Republicans, between Biden or Trump. I mean, by degree, yes, but in principle, no. Because they're all capitalists and capitalism is the machine that will always work towards what is working out now. And we're going into crisis mode again. And of course, it's going to become more authoritarian. And whether the face of authoritarianism is Donald Trump or someone else, it's gonna happen anyway. Even if it comes with a veneer of liberalism, it's still the same thing.

If you look at this historically, after World War Two, we have this extreme rise in productivity. I like to call this age, say, between the 40s and the mid-70s or early 80s, the social democratic era. Because capitalism produced so much productivity, that there was a surplus that could be redistributed. Of course, it was fought over, of course there were still remnants of a working-class movement, or whatever you might want to call it, and the Social Democrat party, but the idea was very strong, even in conservative governments. It was a given that there had to be a redistribution of the wealth that was produced by the productivity surpluses.

BG: *Or a fairer distribution as all this additional wealth and productivity is generated.*

PV: Yeah, exactly. But that has stopped since the first crashes of the 90s. And then, of course, in 2008, when everything went downhill, there were no surpluses. The system is heating up, and there's less to be extracted. And the first thing the system does is to stop the distribution of wealth. So that whole social democratic idea has just been abandoned. And all the people who stood for it, they just changed sides with all these myths, that we have to compete with abroad, and industry is declining, and whatever. All these lies about some structural circumstances that prevent us from keeping on (fairly) distributing the wealth. That's the scene of the moment that we're witnessing. And that means that the living standards of people are going down, especially for the weaker ones, like refugees, like single moms, like working class people. They have to hold down three, four jobs. It's the reality of the post- social democratic era. And in my view, that era was always a scam. I mean, not necessarily with actors behind the scenes who were planning all this. But it was a scam that was coming out of the system because it prevented people from actually working towards a socialist society, because they were okay off, you had benefits and the Social Security system was in place.

And this is all over, and the left abandoned those policies. So, without any answer to the problems on a systemic level—because of course you can't redistribute wealth when there isn't any or when it's hoarded within the one percent—there is no actor to take up that distribution policy. And then the right came in and hijacked that everywhere, Donald Trump does it, all the European countries, the right always claims that they're anti-capitalist, they always sort of pose like that. Of course, it's all a lie, because once they're in power they're the biggest corporate collaborators you could think of.

BG: *Why it is that people are not on the streets with pitchforks saying, we want this fairer distribution of wealth and productivity? Instead of electing George Bush Jr. and Donald Trump whose policies demonstrably increase income inequality?*

PV: I think a lot of it comes down to education. A hundred years ago in Germany, there were lots of clubs or societies organized by the working-class parties and the unions, where people hung out, getting drunk and eating and agitating. This had an educational function. It started in the 19th century, and it went on until, say, the first third of the 20th century. And then with the rise of mass media, radio, TV after World War Two, this was all over. People were fragmented, they stayed at home and of course the official agenda of mass media was not to spread education in socialist terms as these clubs and society would do. The libraries they had going, all that is gone, and people are not interested in that because consuming mass media is much easier. And, now with the internet, there's an additional dimension. It's still corporate bullshit people are consuming, but it's also super fragmented. So there's all this conspiracy stuff coming in. And people are fragmented more than ever, and everybody has their own sense of reality. It's really difficult to aggregate, to get people together to work on something. I think that's the main reason why the powers that be, the forces of capitalism, they see no real resistance. There is resistance, but it's not connected. I see this in Berlin. I'm involved in a couple of initiatives, most of them are based on the tenants movement. Which is one of the strongest angles today in fighting the system.

Because they say, okay, living must be a human right. It's got to be free basically. Which, of course challenges the system at its core. But these initiatives, they're all very tiny, and it is very hard to connect them. Because they are all sort of focused on their sort of micro problems. And at the same time, there is just no time to connect, and to build a wider movement. Apart from say, do that one big demonstration once a year where there's like 25,000 people. That's it, you know. And that's not a real challenge to the system.

And then within that whole fragmentation thing, several progressive movements, all those identity movements. The gay rights movement is super progressive. But now that also has been hijacked and framed in a sort of excessive self, new liberal, shiny, superficial shitshow. And it's no longer challenging the system, but the system has, again pulled that feat, and just sort of integrated these progressive movements and adapted them. So that's it. It's the educational angle, it's fragmentation. And the system has the ability to pull in anything that's sort of progressive and make it their own.

BG: *In the context of today's politics, what was the good German thinking when he or she embraced Adolf Hitler 100 years ago?*

PV: That's a good question. I think a lot of people just thought exactly what you said before, that it's not going to be that bad. People just couldn't fathom what would happen. But then, there were huge demonstrations, like the day before Hitler was elected in early 1933. There were half a million people on the streets of Berlin, demonstrating against this. This was the last demonstration there was until after the war. A lot of people saw this, and that was all the socialists. And I think they saw this because they see that fascism is inherent in capitalism. You can't separate those two. So capitalism is comfortable with social democracy and parliamentary democracy. But only as long as the machine isn't disturbed. And if it is, and that happens automatically, because it goes through these productivity cycles, then it becomes authoritarian, and it has no problem going to bed with guys like Hitler. And there was also a whole class of people like the big landowners in the east that pushed Hitler's agenda because they thought okay, we are in a structural crisis, and this guy is going to help us put the mood down and keep our business intact. And keep our power intact.

BG: *What is your definition of fascism?*

PV: I think one of the key features of fascism is that you play one group of people against another. You elevate one and you treat the others as scum. And blame them for whatever goes wrong. That was the Jews in the 30s. And now it's the Muslims or the liberals or whatever. And that always works very well with your own constituency because it's an identity process. People can think we're the good guys. And these are the bad guys. And that always works very well. But it's running society like a pirate ship. Where the have-nots, the working class, and the refugees or whatever, just to name an example, are fighting each other. And they're being played. And so I think that fascism is the ideology that is at the base of the system. It's playing people against each other.

> *One of the key features of fascism is that you play one group of people against another. You elevate one and you treat the others as scum. And blame them for whatever goes wrong.*

BG: *You've spent your career in advertising. So, Edward Bernays as the Antichrist, true or false?*

PV: Yeah. Definitely true. As an advertising professional, I'm not involved with the content side of things, the brand side. I'm a media planner. I'm dealing with reach levels and frequencies. And

I know that this works: if you push a message—regardless of what message it is—out to people often enough, it becomes part of their reality. Advertising is an interesting thing because I think that it is actually the glue that holds the society together. And it's an ideology that has no active actors, no one in the advertising industry would say this has a social function. They're all car salesmen, they all try to sell their product. But advertising as a whole, it sort of justifies what's going on, it's okay to take a train, it's okay to buy a car, it's okay to eat meat, it's okay to buy women, it's all okay. That is the overall function of advertising. And it works because there's all these miniature pieces that try to sell you something and push it into your brain via lots of contacts. But at the end of the day, it levels the field for capitalism, it suggests that the society we're living in, it's good, consume, consume.

And, of course, that's how fascism works. That's how Hitler came to power. That's how Hitler maintained power. And that's what the right is doing now. They're all on Tik Tok. They're all using these social media channels much better than the left. And the platforms are actually rigged towards that because the algorithms tell you when someone clicks on that, then it gets higher ranked, and it's what you get presented. And that's always the shit you know. Because people click on the clickbait and the right wing's expert in that. It's this endless feedback cycle.

> *I'm a media planner. I'm dealing with reach levels and frequencies. And I know that this works: if you push a message—regardless of what message it is—out to people often enough, it becomes part of their reality.*

CHAPTER 6

AUSTRIA

Vienna Layover

Whereupon I have a Viennese coffee with Austrian publisher Gerhard Oberschlick at Café Landtmann… play a scratched-up vinyl record of Cabaret on my hotel room turntable… and I am told by an Austrian pharmacist and daughter of a high-ranking Nazi officer that Hitler would win in a landslide if he ran today.

GERHARD OBERSCHLICK
You Have to Fight

Gerhard Fritz Oberschlick is an Austrian essayist. A student of German literature, the history of theatre and philosophy at the University of Vienna, he served as editor and owner of the political and cultural magazine FORVM. His rich creative career includes roles as music festival and scientific symposium organizer, literary executor of philosopher Günther Anders, chair of an International Human Rights Tribunal, and dramaturge for plays by Ibsen and Pirandello. During his editorship, FORVM retained its high profile through intellectual and social criticism, avid anti-fascism, and fights for human rights.

GO: We have a pronounced fascist party here. They try to imitate Trump. He is the world's leader of fascism today. And your land and our lands have something in common. We have no law to forbid a fascist party. We have a law against a repetition of national fascism. But when it comes to use this law against the fascist party, they avoid doing it. Trump can run for the presidency again. He's openly fascist. And if he would be convicted, he could still run. That's not the case in Austria.

BG: *That's quite a statement you made, that Trump is the leader of global fascism and that your right-wing parties try to emulate him. What is the appeal for Austrians who adore this man?*

GO: The same that attract them to (Hungarian leader Viktor) Orbán. Illiberal democracy. To find a strongman who leads, a leader with masculinity, who is against homosexuals, against transgenders, against liberals. Strong so you can lay back, and let him do, and if I do nothing, I'm on the safe side.

BG: *Trump says only I can solve your problems. Here we are in Austria, home of Sigmund Freud, who pioneered psychotherapy and the notion that that human beings are motivated by irrational impulses and make decisions based on unconscious fears and repressed aggression. And strongmen, either consciously or by chance, are diabolically successful and effective at harnessing those fears, as you said, to solve your problems.*

GO: It's normal for fascists to kill people. It's normal for fascists not to take care of children from the other colors, to separate families. And if you're not a Jew, and not the colored people, the Nazis said you are Aryan. And for this you are aristocratic in the world. And so the poor people were elevated, I'm an Aryan. This is a chip, a chip to buy the people. The fascists who kill people, who divide the population, this is not the problem, this is normal. The problem is that while the fascists love violence, we liberals avoid it.

BG: *There's a sort of rhetorical or political disadvantage because of the aggressive and dishonest ways that fascists are willing to manipulate people.*

GO: The fascist Trump said I could kill somebody on the street and they would elect me.

BG: *He did say that. I could kill someone on Fifth Avenue.*

GO: He did say it. And he's right. We are waiting till he is president and can make the violence in the world and in the state against his enemies.

BG: *He's publicly promising it.*

GO: Yeah, and we are doing nothing. We have to fight against those who are on the way to kill our democracy.

BG: *Is it surprising to you, after the January 6 assault on the Capitol—I've been in that building many times, it's like a cathedral, a beautiful building—that, four years later, Trump has not been held to account? From your vantage here in Vienna, is this a fundamental flaw and weakness of the American political system?*

GO: Not only the political system in USA. The leftists and the liberals avoid violence from both sides.

BG: *Do you think there should be violence?*

GO: Not the people on the street. The last step, the people on the street. But first, we have institutions. We have police. We have justice. And they should protect democracy.

BG: *And they're not doing it.*

GO: They must put Trump in prison. It's not in the public opinion. Somebody should say it.

BG: *So when you look at this history of the four years Trump was president, and the four years since, do you see similarities to things that happened in Austria and Germany in the past?*

GO: Yeah. Mussolini and Hitler, they were people's leaders. Rhetoric. Hitler wrote what he will do, and he did it. And it was the same as what we see in the USA today. Hitler was elected, democratically elected. Same as Trump. His first term was a democratic election. A system which looks for every vote, the same value, but different weight, because of the Electoral College, because of the different states. So Hillary Clinton had more.

BG: *Yes, she did. Trump has never won an election.*

GO: Trump won the election under the rules of the American system. He would not have won if the system gave every vote the same weight. This is how long, 200 years?

BG: *There's a point of view that the makeup of the United States Senate, the Electoral College and a lot of these systems were put in place by wealthy landowners from the very beginning to be able to have undue influence over the country.*

GO: There had been in the past, a history of leftist factions not avoiding violence. Stalin and now Putin, he is not Marxist, but he is not Western, preying using violence. Our left is not awake enough, but the fascists here are not woke. We are softies.

It makes sense that this boy who shot in the direction of Trump came from the fascist side. It seems he changed his side, but he didn't lose his ability for violence. These are our opponents.

BG: *With climate change and other challenges facing us, is liberal democracy in danger now? Is fascism ascendent?*

GO: Yeah. Democracy is not a radical issue, and the radical speech is winning hearts.

BG: *What's the solution for that?*

GO: I don't know. The soft leftists are thinking about emigration, they don't know where, to which land, a friend of mine told me yesterday, his wife is looking for a house on an island somewhere in the Pacific.

BG: *Sounds great!* (laughs). *So what's needed?*

GO: There is no chance that people would accept antifascist militants to build up. In the 30 years of the last century, the society was divided, and fascists had their own weapons. Here it is not legal. But they do it. Sometimes the police find weapons in right wing societies. The left don't have weapons. Some, there a few anarchists with the ability to fight, but they don't prepare systematically. Systematically, only the rightists fight.

BG: *Do you think that's why in the United States Trump et al are obsessed with antifa, even though there is no organized antifa. It's a few people showing up at a rally to counter armed or aggressive fascists or white supremacists. Do you think they're so obsessed with antifa because they want to block any ability of the left to resist when they get violent?*

GO: Yeah. That is the situation.

BG: *So if Trump were elected again, what would you expect in the United States?*

GO: He will appoint his Proud Boys and other Trumpists to positions in the state. He will demolish the justice system, bringing it under his control. What he will do in USA is one thing, what he will do with NATO is another.

MARIA H.
The Pharmacist's Daughter

Maria is a well-traveled Austrian author of retirement age who carries on the professional tradition of her family, owning and managing pharmacies spanning the past half century.

BG: *What interests me is, what was the appeal of Nazism? You said that Germans and Austrians regretted what happened because they lost the war, not because of anything Hitler did.*

MH: After the First World War, all was destroyed. And then Hitler came and said, there will be work and the youth will grow, and we will build up all again. And he did. Yes. Everybody loved him because he was a very good speaker with very good ideas. And also, we are Aryan, you know. And we really were more educated.

BG: *Germany was one of the most advanced civilizations in the world with opera, with architecture, with education, a very advanced European culture.*

MH: And the Jewish came and take over this. Especially you see in Vienna, where they live, they had their own properties and they were very rich because they took the people, they took the money by cheating from us. It was not a nice thing what they did, so nobody liked them. Yes, because they were cheating in everything. So Hitler's ideas to make Aryan society, everybody found were good. War is not nice and if they burn the Jewish in Yugoslavia, they raped all women, it's war. You cannot do something good in war. No.

BG: *So was there a point with the concentration camps, with invading Poland…*

MH: We didn't even know about it.

BG: *Didn't know about it?*

MH: No.

BG: *It was hidden from…*

MH: It was hidden. I just read that near where I was born, where our pharmacies were, there was a very big concentration camp. I didn't know it. In the south of Austria, where I was born. It's still there. A young man who is looking into this, he wrote a few books. I don't know on which side he is. If he's on the Hitler side or on the other side, I don't know. Because you have to be careful. If you say something against it, you are racist, and you have problems in Austria. But we Austrians, we speak about it. But we are wondering that others think we are all bad people, because Nazis were not bad people. No.

BG: *You married an East African guy. So how racist can you be?* (laughs)

MH: Right? (*laughs*)

BG: *Right. You must be a very progressive woman. Was there a time, 1939 or whenever with the military actions into Czechoslovakia and Poland, and then into Russia, and some of the more aggressive rallies* *and speeches, Kristallnacht and the attacks on Jews, was there a time that some Austrians at that time were starting to say, whoa, maybe we should reconsider this fellow?*

MH: No.

BG: *They were like, it's all good.*

MH: They think we will win.

BG: *And they're not concerned about any of those…*

MH: No. Because Hitler till the end, till Stalingrad, he said, "We are Aryan." Although already it was all kaput. But people believed in him. In his ideas, he made very interesting surgeries. Not with disabled people. He tested many things on this pharmaceutically.

BG: *Was your father's pharmaceutical company involved in any of those?*

MH: Yes.

BG: *They were?*

MH: We had all these morphine products as a big pharmacy. And my father was a morphinist. And my grandfather was on cocaine. I think we stored all this because the injured people needed this. At that time there was no paper to do.

BG: *But there was no pharmaceutical support for like the gas chambers or any of that stuff. Your family was not providing any technology or equipment for any of that?*

MH: I don't know.

BG: *You don't know? Or can't say. (laughs). You said your father gave himself a golden shot.*

MH: He was 40 years old. He was just overwhelmed with his marriage, with his financial problems, with his drug abuse. He was also alcoholic. I was 11 years old. 1960s already.

BG: *He had no regret about Hitler or supporting Nazis?*

MH: No. No, no regret.

BG: *Was there at all a feeling in Austria, even though Hitler was Austrian, we don't want the Germans taking over our country. Was there resistance?*

MH: No. The Germans was our friends. It's not that they had to invite us. No, we went.

BG: *Was Austria as damaged as Germany in World War Two?*

MH: Yes, there was nothing anymore. It was strange that this part where I'm born, there was no damage. I think because they are the bosses. The bosses were protected.

BG: *Today, in Austria, there are right-wing, anti-immigrant politicians. How widespread do you think fondness or affection for Nazism or Hitler is there in Austria today?*

MH: One hundred percent.

BG: *That's a big percent.*

MH: Because now in Austria, we live like guests. And the rest are immigrants. So they get everything from the government. And our people who are retired, they suffer. They don't have enough to eat. Because all the money goes to these people. We don't have Austria anymore. Before we had Italy, Yugoslavia, Germany. Now we have a mixture of something.

BG: *In the past, were there migrant workers?*

MH: We had the Italians. We had the Yugoslavians. We had these waves. Then the Turkish. And especially the Turkish bring problems. Because they are very different in character.

BG: *In the recent elections, the right-wing parties have been strong, yes?*

MH: Yeah. It must not be a Hitler, but a kind of Hitler. A kind of Hitler who makes order again. Who makes it organized again. Now, we as Austrians are not even heard. Now you have to go to a security check like in an airport, because the immigrants go with their pistols! If they don't get served immediately, they shoot! You cannot go out in the evening as a woman with a short dress, they come and take you.

BG: *They come and take you.*

MH: The Turkish.

BG: *If you were to look at Austria now, with the problems that you describe, what policies of the Nazi party from the 1930s would you change if you were going to reintroduce them? Or, just let's do the same thing as they did in the 1930s?*

MH: Not the same thing. You cannot put all people in one pot because they are too different. We are not used to Europeans. We are used to Austrians, Germans, Italians. So for us they are different. And now we should be all Europeans. But I'm not Yugo-slavian. I'm not.

BG: *You don't like the European Union?*

MH: No, I'm still working as a pharmacist, and my problem with the immigrants is they say, "I don't have money." And excuse me, the medicine, somebody has to pay. They say, "I don't pay. The government pay," then I say, "I cannot give you," and then the story starts. So I have to close, so I don't get a pistol on my nose.

BG: *Are there are a lot of people who have been shot in Austria by immigrants?*

MH: They don't make it in the paper. No. Because what the immigrants do, they can go without ticket somewhere. Nothing will happen. They don't work. Nothing will happen. They make wrong certificates. All good. If you do it as an Austrian, you get prison. So there are two measurements now. And when I don't give this medicine in the night to this man or woman, I am in trouble.

BG: *What law are you breaking?*

MH: I break the law that these immigrants are allowed everything. They get paid. They get paid the house, they get paid the petrol, the phone, smartphone, whatever. They get paid everything. Why shall they pay medicine?

We lost our jobs in Austria. And now the Bulgarians and Romanians take our jobs. It started with the Jewish people. And it goes now to other populations.

BG: *Well, I think Hitler didn't like the Romani people very much either.*

MH: You're right, you're right. When you live in Europe, if you go to Poland, your car is already there. You know what it means?

BG: *No.*

MH: It means they're stealing cars. The Polish people. So they say you don't have to go with your car to Poland. Your car is already there. It is true. If I go Autobahn, I see pickup trucks with three, four cars. You know what they do? They steal. If you say I want a Mercedes 380. They go look, steal, and then deliver.

BG: *So the current right-wing political parties in Austria…*

MH: They will get more and more.

BG: *What do they want?*

MH: They want really to put the immigrants back where they came from. But will not be possible. There are too many. You know, Africans come every weekend, the ships still come to Lampedusa (the largest of the Italian Pelagie Islands in the Mediterranean) with I don't know how many thousands. Every weekend, but they don't show it anymore on TV because the Austrians are mad. And they say, send them back. Turn the ship and send them back. But then I am racist.

BG: *You said almost all, or most, the vast majority of Germans and Austrians did not know about concentration camps. If they did know…?*

MH: Doesn't care.

BG: *They wouldn't care.*

MH: No. Because they would say they were bad. It's okay. So when I speak with people, we just speak in a small round. You cannot speak it somewhere because if you are racist then you get really in trouble. I don't know if you pay or go to prison, I may lose my license.

BG: *In Germany I know there's some laws against promotion of National Socialism or Hitler. Probably similar in Austria.*

MH: Sure. Same thing.

—

Besides my Viennese mélange with Gerhard at Café Landtmann, my brief overnight on my first visit to my grandfather Sam Gruber's hometown features a Mozart concert at Musikverein's Golden Hall, a stay at Jaz in the City hotel which offers a free library of vinyl recordings to be played on turntables provided in each room (I choose the Cabaret soundtrack, George Benson, and Sting), and rooftop cocktails round midnight for a meditative look at the skyline and reflections on my Germany and Austria visits.

CHAPTER 7

HUNGARY

Orbán's Illiberal Democracy

Whereupon I am hosted for dinner at Gettó Gulyás with a media official and diplomat of the Orbán government… eat Hungarian pancakes with Miklos outside the House of Terror, followed by an evening walking tour of Hungarian history… and wander to the basement of Europe's largest synagogue for the story of Hungary's collaboration with Nazi Germany in the mass deportation and murder of their Jewish population.

PETER BAKONYI

A Culture of Identity

Peter Bakonyi asks where I might like to meet and I request something uniquely Hungarian. Gettó Gulyás is his choice, a popular spot in the Jewish Quarter, near Europe's largest synagogue. And while I intend to opt for the obvious choice of Hungarian goulash on my first night in Budapest, he steers me to other options. He is a thoughtful and engaging dinner companion, generous with his time and opinions. I have heard a lot of criticism of the Viktor Orbán regime in the United States and am eager to hear his views on Hungarian politics and his country's experience with fascist, communist, and other forms of authoritarianism.

PB: I mainly work in the media. I am the head of the press department of the Hungarian Academy of Arts right now. Before that, I worked in Hungarian public television, I was editor-in-chief. Right before that, between 2014 and '18, I was the Consul General for Hungary in Melbourne, Australia. And before that, I was the programming director of the Hungarian public channel. I've worked in the political area, then mostly the cultural areas.

BG: *So as you saw Viktor Orbán enter the public sphere, what were your initial thoughts as you saw him as a leader, as a personality? What interested you about him?*

PB: What I remember, in 1989 and I was 13 years old, there was the rehabilitation of the former Hungarian Prime Minister who led the Hungarian Revolution in 1956. And there was a re-burying, it was a huge mass action with 100,000 people on the Heroes Square in the center of Budapest, and I was there in the first line, and there was Viktor Orbán, who started to speak. It was a very revolutionary speech, never forgot it. One year before all the changes, Russian soldiers were still in Hungary. And after a while, he just said, 'We want you out, all the Russian soldiers, go home and leave our country'. And I was standing there with open mouth. I was a very political kid with my mom, everywhere, all the demonstrations, running from the cops and police. It was in 1987, '88–'89. So, he was a kind of superhero in my eyes. Somebody who finally said, 'Russian soldiers get out of our country'.

BG: *In '56, you mean the PM was the one deposed?*

PB: In '56, when the revolution started, Imre Nagy became prime minister after the previous Prime Minister had run away. The people accepted him because he stepped on the side of the revolutionary people. And he said, okay, 'I'm here for you, we'll have our own new government and the Russians should go home'. And that was the big '56 revolution. He became prime minister for two weeks. Then the Russians came back and killed him.

The Hungarian popular uprising in 1956 followed a speech by Soviet leader Nikita Khrushchev denouncing Joseph Stalin, who died in March of 1953. Rebels won an agreement from the government to establish a multiparty system. On November 4, the USSR invaded Hungary to stop the revolution, resulting in the deaths of more than 2,500 Hungarians.

BG: *So Orbán has a history with the Russian presence.*

PB: In 1989, he was around 22 years old, after university. His speech included that the Russians go. He said the same as the prime minister had in 1956. It was a big deal. they wrote about it all over the world. That the young Hungarian politician said that the Russians should go home from Eastern Europe. So he was a big superhero for me.

BG: *As a 13-year-old, what was your perception about the presence of the USSR in Hungary?*

PB: As kids we were always trying to tease the soldiers, we went behind them and tried to throw small stones at them. So it was small revolutions every day for kids who were actively involved in politics, but we thought they were gonna stay for a long, long time. We could have not imagined that in one year time they will be all gone. And it happened more than two decades before I was born. So we thought that's how it is. We are under pressure from a huge Soviet Union power, and we will always stay there and be slaves. As a 13-year-old, I thought that maybe when I will be grown up and an old person, maybe we can do something to get those people out. We could have not even dreamed about one year.

BG: *Up until the time the Russians left, in what form were Hungarians resisting? Or were they, after 1956?*

PB: All the universities had different groups. And there was a center of it in a small village Lakitelek. That we should somehow stop this and make a new free country of Hungary. And most of these people that started there knew each other and they started to organize demonstrations on the streets. After a while there were hundreds of thousands of people with candles in their hands and singing. And no aggressive crash with the police. Sometimes small ones. But not big ones. I've seen with my eyes when they beat Viktor Orbán on the corner, I was just ten meters from him, they were hitting, kicking him on the ground.

BG: *What's the relationship now between Hungary and Russia? Is there a residual resentment or resistance among Hungarians after all those years of repression?*

PB: I think mine is the youngest generation who still have some negative feelings about the Russians because we lived in it. So we've got experience in it, and those who knew more about the history about the last century have some negative feelings about it. But the youngest, I'm 48, so those under 40, I don't think they think about Russians as different from any other countries, other people in Europe. So I don't think there will be any problem now. It's pretty practical. People don't hate Russians, even if there is the war. Everybody mostly think that it's a terrible thing that they did. It was a terrible decision from Vladimir Putin that they attacked a neighboring country and they did what they did. But in general, they have no problems with the Russians. So if they've got a

Russian singer in a theater, a Russian movie, or a Russian sports man in their soccer team, they don't do what others do in other Western countries. So we don't hate Russians. We hate that thing that Putin did with his army because it happened to us before. So we know how bad it is, and how bad it must be for the Ukrainians. So we feel with the Ukrainians, absolutely.

But we are against the sanctions. Most of the people are against them. At the beginning, they thought that it might be good, because these economic sanctions against Russia might change their mind and pull their army back. But we have realized, it's just bad for us. We've seen the numbers, after every sanction, it was just better for Russia and worse for the European Union. We didn't have oil, gas, it was just so expensive. All the inflation started. So after the course of sanctions, we said that, 'Okay, it's tough enough. It didn't work. Let's do something else. Let's go back to normal.' And we really didn't want to get involved in this war, because we are a neighboring country. Our economy is just so hard to keep it on a level, or it's going down because of the European Union sanctions. And we are just getting closer and closer to the war, that we really don't want, it's not our enemy. It's two countries' problem. We're trying to help the Ukrainians refugees and the Ukrainians there. So it's the biggest humanitarian action we have ever done in our history. Hungarians are very much feeling with Ukrainians and helping them, but we don't want to feel that it's our world. We are not attacked. Ukraine is not a part of NATO. NATO is not attacked.

BG: *This phrase that you hear about, taken originally from a Fareed Zakaria essay when he edited* Foreign Affairs *magazine, illiberal democracy. What does that mean to you?*

PB: It has a totally different meaning in Hungary and in Central Europe than it could mean in Western countries, or especially in the States. Illiberal is for us the opposite of liberal, in a political sense. If you ask somebody in this area of the world what liberal means, they would probably say that it's pretty much a synonym of woke, gender, all this stuff.

And if somebody says here that it's illiberal, it says that as an anti-woke agenda. Liberal, word is from liberty, from freedom. You could imagine that illiberal means against freedom and against liberty. It's against a political way of thinking, it's a political agenda.

BG: *There are criticisms that over the years, Orbán's party has restricted the ability of people to engage in political opposition. Limits on media ownership. You've heard it all. Is it unfair?*

PB: It's unfair because there is nothing to it. In the Hungarian media, officially and scientifically, proof, it's something like 55% is the opposition and 45% is the government. The most problem is that the public television and public radio channels are totally in the government's hands. Yes, as it has always been before in the leftist and the liberals' time. But, if you check the reach and how many people those mediums reach, it's more than half is in hand of the opposition. So it's mathematically incredible what they're saying. On the other hand, even in the public media, every time the opposition has the chance to say, they can go in, they're invited. It's very often happening, I've worked there. Very often, we sent 30 invitations, and they didn't come. And they came the 31st time. And they said you haven't invited us for half a year, then we showed the emails that we did. But they wanted to have this image to stay on the surface. So the public media is the government's. I wouldn't even say it's very powerful though, hardly any people watching because it's not that popular, because it's boring. So most of the people watch the opposition versions of it. It's something like in a balance, but still the balance is on the opposition side. So it's obviously not true. You can go on the streets, there are demonstrations on the streets all the time, every medium is talking about it. I just say come to Hungary and check it. Turn on the TV, watch the online sites, I can tell you ten leftie online sites and maybe three or five right ones, so we don't have balance problems here. But it sounds good.

BG: *What appealed to CPAC, the Conservative Political Action Committee, about what Orbán was doing such that they would hold their annual meeting here?*

PB: I myself didn't understand it, that a huge country's political power would come here. It's probably simply because we could be what Silicon Valley is for IT people, could be this very small Budapest or Hungary for political right-wing people, because it's small, not that big. But still, extremely successful. And totally not totalitarian. It's simply democratic, illiberal democratic because it's the other way, it's not the mainstream. It's working. If it works in a small version, why wouldn't it work in a big one? And it's consequential and true, what Orbán is saying all the time. He's always said the same thing. We don't want a big war; we don't want illegal migrants.

BG: *There's a perception, as you know, that there's a xenophobic, anti-Muslim, possibly racist attitude towards certain ethnic groups that Orbán gins up.*

PB: We are in the Jewish district now. Just go out and look around, Jewish, Muslims, black people, everything. I've never experienced any problems. It's not that somebody doesn't like another race or something. But there is a culture of identity of this country. We have the right to decide, as the Germans do, whether we want to change this old cultural integrity and identity or not. You can say, yeah, let's make a multicultural country out of it, as the United

States, Australia is, now France and Germany is like that. It's totally multicultural, very different colors. But if you say no, we are happy to stay like this, as Japanese say or Saudi Arabians do. Have you ever heard about people migrating to Saudi Arabia? No. Are you angry about it? No. It's their country. It's their right. It's not fascistic. It's not Nazi. Not racist to say that this is our country, we'd like it stay like this. We'd like to keep it culturally clean like that. We accept a certain number of refugees. We don't hate them. If you walk as a Muslim, you will never have a racist problem in Hungary, you can go at midnight, anytime. So it's not racism. It's just an identity. For us, it's okay. For an American, it might not be okay.

We didn't colonize the world. We didn't have slaves. We didn't mistreat any other races. We didn't have problems with Indians just to get their land. So you've got different problems, different backgrounds, we don't have those. This is why these things are not an issue for us. So that's why we don't care about it. I don't think most Hungarians are homophobic. It's somehow harder to understand, sometimes it's not tasteful for heterosexuals to see homosexuals to kiss each other. The problem is not with liberating them. The problem is with this extremely crazy exaggerating of these things. You cannot watch a Netflix or Amazon movie without having a homosexual in it. It's just too much. Angry people are coming out of the cinema sometimes, asking why does the hero always have to be a homosexual guy, and the heterosexual white 50 year old male is the bad guy? We are just fed up with it.

It's the same with feminism. As long as feminism was about having the same rights, equality, it was a great idea. But nowadays, when the feminists would like to have 90 percent quotas, they want to be men, now not for me in 2024. Feminists who I talk to usually hate women. Because they say that only male characteristics are something to respect. And this is why they want to be very masculine in their clothes, dressing, hairstyle, muscles, all the stuff.

And when I say that, for me, it's so beautiful to have a lady without tattoos, without big muscles, then they think I'm an anti-feminist, homophobic whatever. No. As soon as they reach the same rights, the same salaries, everything is equal. For me, feminism reached its aim. It's over. There is no more need for feminism. But they didn't want to stop there. They want more and more. Having a man between women in a running competition, it's not feminism, it's not LGBT issues, it's just crazy. It's not fair. That's what I'm saying. I am a feminist because that's against the female people. It's too much for most us in Hungary.

BG: *Orbán seems to like Trump a lot. Trump seems to like Orbán a lot. What's your perception of Trump as a political leader?*

PB: Trump is good for Hungarians. That's why we are on his side. If Trump will be the president, Hungary will win all these questions we were talking about. If he's not winning, we are losing. That's why we are with him because he is with us. But we have no right to tell you anything about it.

MIKLOS MARTIN-KOVACS
Goulash Authoritarianism

Miklos Martin-Kovacs is a veteran broadcast, TV and online journalist, foreign correspondent, media entrepreneur, yoga instructor, and professionally trained baker.

I meet Miklos in a cafe fronting the House of Terror, a museum documenting the fascist and communist regimes of 20th century Hungary while commemorating its victims.

Miklos promises to take me on a walking tour of Hungarian historical monuments and spaces. For now, he orders Hungarian pancakes for us as we settle in for our conversation.

MMK: I went to the States in 1990 as a visiting fellow, the national foundation based in Washington D.C. had a wonderful idea to bring to the states, a group of people from Poland, the Czech Republic, and Hungary. Maybe 15 of us were invited, we went for 15 weeks. They assigned those of us in the media to two places, C-SPAN was one. It was an amazing firsthand experience, understanding the mechanism of Congress and the political class in the U.S.

BG: *What was the experience like for you coming out of Hungary?*

MMK: It was a life changing experience, literally. Watching the world from behind the Iron Curtain, even if Hungary was a goulash communism country, so it wasn't as bad when I grew up. I didn't experience many of the horrors that previous generations experienced.

BG: *Was that because it was the post-Stalin era?*

MMK: Yes, they were the personal cult years and that's why the revolution in 1956 happened. I was four, so I don't have direct memories from those years. After that, the Soviets dominated the political class and the one-party system tried to please a lot of the population. They weren't very harsh. Hungary was in a way a mecca compared to the Czech Republic, or Eastern Germany, not to mention the Soviet Union. I had international experience before in Western and Eastern Europe, I was a professional hand-ball player. We traveled with the team to different places, but I had never been to the U.S.

BG: *When I was in Kyiv a few years ago, Ukrainians seemed to under-stand and appreciate liberal democracy, the rule of law more than Americans, because it was new to them. And because they understood that contrast. What was your perception of American democracy?*

MMK: First of all, the history. Of course, we knew about the Reagan, Mr. Gorbachev ('Tear down that wall') moment. And the importance of the Anglo-Saxon presence in the international arena. I knew about from newspapers and magazines, though as a newcomer I didn't sense any of the controversial and nasty parts of American politics. And then I didn't know about the real meaning of the race issues in the U.S.

BG: *What is Viktor Orbán's appeal to the Hungarian people?*

MMK: That's a very interesting story. I was hoping you would ask because I'm old enough to have seen the whole evolution. There was an opportunity for the opposition to form an anticommunist coalition and that led to a free election. Viktor Orbán was one of the young heroes and they founded their party, the Free Democrats party, and he played a major role. He was just really a role model for many, for the young and for the older generation. He was kind of a hope, that okay, now the new generation is coming, and these kinds of people are going to lead Hungary into modern democracy. The elections happened in 1990 and an old type of Conservative Party won. Basically, they formed a government and that government didn't want to do anything with Viktor Orbán because he was a liberal. So he didn't have a place. He found himself in a weird situation because he was obviously anticommunist as much as anybody could be. But he spent the first four years in opposition, and after four years, for some very interesting reasons, he was the Young Democrats party leader, he was left out of power again. So another four years passed, and in the meantime, used the advice of Hungarian politicians on immigration, and kind of realized that, wait a minute, with that kind of policy, he's not gonna get anywhere.

BG: *What was the policy profile that he was representing at that time?*

MMK: He wasn't a major player. Hundreds of new laws were introduced, the country was getting the legal system ready for the European Union. That was probably a very bitter experience for him. But he was a strategist, he realized he had to figure something out. So he went to the conservative side and surrounded himself with advisers and built up a new strategy. And in 1998, his party won. So although he had to form a coalition, he became prime minister in 1998. So that was a victory for Viktor, it was an amazing opportunity for him. But they lost the following election. And that lasted for another eight years. And those eight years were really important, because they very consciously built up a new political strategy for themselves. They educated their people. They realized how much they had to change pretty much everything if they were to win again. For eight years, they built up a shadow state. The whole concept. And then people were educated who joined this whole idea, they knew who was going to be their government, the ministers and what they were going to do. And in 2010, they finally won again. And that was a big opportunity, so they immediately changed the constitution, because they won the majority, not just the simple majority, but the two thirds in parliament. So could do anything they wanted, even if it wasn't legal, it became legal in two days, because they just introduced a new law and they accepted it in parliament.

BG: *People in power do things when they're in power. Pushing the envelope a little. As opposed to this being the beginning of a dismantling of the guardrails of democracy in order to maintain power. How does one understand this as simple power politics versus the beginning of a slide towards authoritarianism?*

MMK: I'm not an expert on fascism, but I think what's present in fascism is the control of the state over everything, over institutions, over the different kind of nominations, the judiciary system, the constitutional court, the financial system, and the media. I think that was designed this way when this government came into power in 2010. Hungary was and is a member of the European Union and NATO. It's kind of a very interesting game in a way to act as if it was a completely democratic country. The whole process is justified as representing national interests and running against the overwhelming influence of multinational companies. They reorganized how we arrange everything, and it was computerized, so it serves better, but it also gives a very excellent opportunity to control and the institutions were very much reshaped. And if there was a new law needed to do that, it was possible because of the two thirds majority in the parliament.

BG: *Was there popular enthusiasm for what he was doing? And was the viable opposition being diminished by efforts to limit the ability of people to run against him?*

MMK: It wasn't done like in Russia, with Putin. Viktor Orbán is an extremely talented politician and he thinks long term. He's trying to position it as, this is a small country, not very powerful economically, militarily. He says we have to gain what we can in the international arena. And as with most authoritarian leaders, he probably believes that this is the only way he can do it, because his whole concept of the illiberal democracy is pretty much against the western style of democracy. This is the only way a country can run against the multinational financial conglomerates and that's why they pick George Soros as an arch enemy. In the meantime, let's not forget about the fact that Hungary is a new member of the European Union and, during these 20 years, a huge amount of development money pours into the country, and even if Hungary had issues with the European Union, the government wanted to make sure most of that money goes into ventures that do the job, but support and strengthen the current government and members of the elite.

BG: *Outside of his simply being a politician going his own way, trying to get things done, what concerns you about Orbán?*

MMK: Whatever he wants, it happens. It was 14 years ago when they won the elections. And ever since we have never experienced a debate between an official opposition leader and Orbán. There's no public platform for the people to see who thinks what, who has what kind of arguments. That's one of the main concerns that a system like this, even if there's no torture, no Navalny type of issues, they don't smash political parties. It's not like that. The whole system represents this government's interests and views. This is the way how you pretend this is a working democracy. But in real terms, it's not. As far as the media is concerned, there is a state-owned part of the public media. The other media organizations, there are a few independent media outlets. They can be pretty well presented, especially in the online sphere. But most of the regional newspapers and TV and radio stations were consolidated and transferred into one company. It's not state owned. It's privately owned. But it's dominated by the state. And the Hungarian official news agency, even with soft methods, makes sure most of the people only get the message they want them to get.

BG: *Are there elections where opposition can effectively challenge Orbán?*

MMK: The opposition doesn't have the financial backing to build and run a powerful operation. I think the opposition slowly, year by year, became weaker and weaker intellectually as well. Hungary is a small country, but Budapest is a major hub with two million people, the other eight million people live in the countryside, and the opposition doesn't really get to them with their messages because it costs a lot of money. They don't have their channels; they don't have their publications. They are powerless in this respect.

BG: *Is there political repression in the form of prisoners, torture, exile, imprisonment, murder?*

MMK: I mean I don't know about it. From this respect, this is the European Union and NATO. It could happen if somebody is very active, that the tax authority might show increasing interest.

BG: *Is there a term that you would use to describe this form of governance?*

MMK: It's authoritarian, but if you say that, you immediately identify it with the big guys, the big authoritarian leaders. And this is different. So, yes, it's a Hungarian version. I haven't thought of this, but ironically, just like communism was sort of a Hungarian style of communism, I think this might be an authoritarian system, Hungarian style.

BG: *Are there active socialist or communist parties in Hungary?*

MMK: Yes. The Socialist Party is losing power dramatically. During this European Union election a couple of weeks ago they hardly survived. So, they are there, but there is one very small party. Not significant. Nobody cares. What is significant though, we mentioned George Soros, which shows when the system wants to do something, to make sure nothing really challenges the whole system, then serious things could happen. I wouldn't have thought that the Central European University, which was founded by George Soros decades ago and became a very successful university, could be just pushed out of the country. And they were pushed out.

There was one radio station that was openly antigovernment and at a very good level, high-level public radio system and programming. And they turned to the public to support them, to fund them, and the public did. You have to apply for the renewal of broadcast licenses. And for some interesting reasons, their application wasn't successful and they went to court. And of course, they went through the whole court system, two levels, three levels, and they lost everything, every court case. Of course they are doing their programming online so they do exist, but they disappeared from the airwaves.

BG: *The government drove the Open Society organization out of Hungary, so why the obsession with George Soros?*

MMK: There was a serious political fight. There was a Norwegian fund, the Norwegian government offers money to organizations and that's pretty much great. They cannot continue that because the Norwegian government didn't let the Hungarian government control where the money goes. They found an innovation that was done to make sure the money went to different NGOs and the government refused. So the society is pretty much this way. Many of the NGOs just disappeared. And so these little things, this is not something where they're gonna open fire on somebody, but they're gonna stop it.

It's not a direct censorship but they can just evaluate where they get their resources from, how they compose their content, and so it's kind of a very dangerous area again.

They built a wall between Hungary and Serbia, and partially between Hungary and Croatia, because the south was the main route for the migrants, like 200 kilometers, but in the middle of the European Union, and we had the Schengen and we are enjoying the benefits of the free travel. And that's a major thing, let me tell you, it's amazing that we are having it. We are members of the European Union. We are European.

They certainly want to emphasize and make sure Hungary is perceived as a Christian dominated country. Of course, anybody can have any kind of religion, but the country, per se, follows the

Christian tradition. And that's what they support and encourage, this is an important element of his whole concept.

BG: *I saw a couple of posters on street corners with picture of Trump after he got shot holding up his fist. I don't know what it was advertising. Maybe it was a media promotion. Orbán just went to meet with Trump, an unusual thing to do, I think, for a head of state, to someone who is out of power. Why do they like each other so much?*

MMK: I think it's an old story. And from Viktor Orbán's perspective, it's a very successful political PR campaign, because he's the prime minister of a small central European country. The Democrat administration didn't respect, and even criticized the Orbán government's actions, and the prime minister was never invited to the Obama White House. On the other hand, during the Trump years, they found common ground. Just like Trump had favorites in the authoritarian world, it was obvious that the system that was developed and carefully designed here, would be nice for Trump in the U.S. The Hungarian government developed a presence in the U.S. through lobbyists and maybe through institutional contact and the Danube Institute. When I was in Washington in 1990, the Heritage Foundation was a very respected, serious conservative think tank, like the Cato Institute. And then I realized, wait a minute, they are taking the advice of the Hungarian government. Project 2025 built in several ideas and practices from the Hungarian government, so Viktor Orbán made himself a serious player on a global level this way. And hundreds of millions of dollars' worth of marketing value were there when everybody kept talking about Viktor Orbán. Eight years ago, nobody would have known who Viktor Orbán was. Now everybody knows.

BG: *You had an experience seeing American democracy up close, you've been involved in media and observing world politics for decades. With* *your experience with Orbán, what would concern you about a Trump re-election in the United States?*

MMK: I think the whole program, especially the program that was explained in Project 2025, is based on a much more powerful presidency. And that would automatically mean that the institutions would be weakened. The control would be complete and staffing would be based on loyalty. I think these things would have global impact. I would be very concerned about the Supreme Court, I would be very concerned about human rights, the healthcare system, I would be very concerned about the fact that they wouldn't put a lot of effort into developing a viable childcare system in the United States. I couldn't even imagine the horror of gathering millions of illegal immigrants and deporting them. It's just awful. And altogether, I think the political style that is based on verbal attacks, with no respect for doing things on a very high moral level, everything would be very concerning.

> *Project 2025 is based on a much more powerful presidency. And that would mean that the institutions would be weakened.*
>
> *The control would be complete and staffing would be based on loyalty. I think these things would have global impact.*

We leave the café and Miklos drives us to the Hungarian Parliament area, replete with numerous statues and historically significant landmarks. We spend the next hour walking the neighborhood.

MMK: Orbán didn't feel Hungary was treated with respect in the EU, so he created a right-wing faction in the European Parliament. Marine Le Pen, the Austrians, it's now a political home for him.

His party was pushed out of the traditional conservative faction. He is trying to make himself important on a European level. Many things here in the past two decades were financed by the European Union. A small country has to be tricky to save its respect and dignity. The EU did not appreciate the legal framework his government developed.

Miklos is looking for parking. We discuss the advantages of life without a car. He tells me that bicycling has become more popular in Budapest. I mention how impressed I was with Munich, with bike paths sharing sidewalks everywhere I went.

MMK: I don't think Hungarians have much affection for Trump, at all, but the United States and our government are at odds. Orbán often publishes support for Trump on his Facebook page. 'We are crossing our fingers for you, Mister President. We hope you are going to win.' He combines Trump's name with the prospect of peace with Ukraine. He declares that only Trump could make peace.

BG: *You had a historically unpleasant relationship with Moscow. Now he is friendly with Putin.*

MMK: Each government needed a cordial relationship with Russia because of the oil and gas supply; we are dependent. This government has developed a special relationship. No one knows what it is about beyond the oil and gas issue. Putin didn't go anywhere but he came here. Orbán went to Moscow. The Russians built the first nuclear power station here and they're building a second which will cover 50 percent of Hungarian electric supply.

BG: *Orbán and Putin present themselves as the protectors of Caucasian Christian civilization.*

MMK: Behind this building is a square with a statue. Miklós Horthy was the governor before the second world war, that was the PM title. He took Hungary into the war with the Germans. He tried to escape from the German alliance but couldn't. Was still in power in 1944 when the Germans invaded and installed a fascist government and then the Holocaust in Hungary happened. He escaped and went to Portugal and spent the rest of this life there. After the war, he was not a welcome figure in public policy, considered a war criminal by the communists. Nothing good about him in the history books. And responsible for 200,000 Hungarian soldiers lost in the war.

BG: *Why is Trianon mentioned on the bust?*

MMK: The winners of World War One took two thirds of Hungary in (the Treaty of) Trianon. The nationalistic right wing wanted to bring him back to honor him as a hero of Hungary. Public opinion was not favorable and they did not allow the statue, so this church allowed this show of respect but not in a public space.

BG: *The church gives him that privilege, saying what about the church?*

MMK: The church does whatever they want to do.

BG: *Were they complicit with the Nazis?*

MMK: They were not against per se.

BG: *Hungary did not deport Jews until the Germans took over.*

MMK: They tried to avoid that.

BG: *Antisemitic but not quite as bloodthirsty.*

MMK: A prime minister (Pál Teleki) committed suicide because he could not manage to keep Hungary out of the German alliance.

—⁓—

I walk back to the Jewish Quarter, getting accosted by numerous tourist restaurant hawkers.

I passed the Dohany Street synagogue several times during my Budapest visit. It is a grand structure, the largest synagogue in Europe. The onion-shaped domes with gilded ornaments are unusual for their Moorish aesthetics. Stone tablets with the 10 Commandments are placed at the top. Behind the arc of the synagogue is a huge organ. Franz Liszt performed at its opening ceremony on September 6, 1859. Named after its street, it is also known as the great or main synagogue. It is among the top 10 tourist sights of Budapest. The current structure was completed in 1931. The synagogue houses both a Jewish museum, holding artworks, books of scripture, and historic artifacts, and a Holocaust exhibition.

The Soviet Army liberated Budapest on January 18, 1945, ending a reign of terror by the fascist, pro-Nazi Arrow Cross. Thousands had starved during a siege of the Jewish quarter. Two thousand, two hundred eighty-one victims are buried in mass graves in the garden behind the synagogue. Many are commemorated by plaques with names of the dead. Many remain unnamed. Below the synagogue is an exhibition in remembrance of the victims of Hungary's fascist government and Nazi occupation. Photos of normal street life in the vibrant Jewish quarter from the 1920s look similar to life in Jewish immigrant neighborhoods from Manhattan's Lower East Side. The exhibits grow darker with the enactment of anti-Jewish laws, with young women wearing large yellow Jewish stars on their dresses, scenes of deportations and mass killings, forced marches, and attacks by Arrow Cross members.

The synagogue was bombed by the Arrow Cross Party on February 3, 1939. It was later used as a base for German radio transmissions as well as stables. From May 15 to July 9, 1944, Hungarian police, under the direction of German SS officers, deported around 440,000 Jews, most to the Auschwitz-Birkenau concentration camp, for extermination in gas chambers. Thousands of others were sent to Austria for forced labor, digging fortification trenches. By the end of the war, an estimated 565,000 Hungarian Jews had been murdered.

Outside the building, a park honors Swedish diplomat Raoul Gustaf Wallenberg. As an envoy stationed in Budapest, he saved thousands of Jews between July and December 1944 by issuing passports and protecting them in buildings which he declared as Swedish territory. On January 17, 1945, during the siege of Budapest by the Red Army, he was detained by the Soviets on suspicion of espionage. In 1957, 12 years after his disappearance, he died while imprisoned in Lubyanka prison in Moscow.

ERIC ALTERMAN
The Fight for Liberalism

Eric Alterman is a CUNY Distinguished Professor of English and Journalism. He was the media columnist for *The Nation* for 25 years, now a columnist for The American Prospect, and is the author of twelve books. He has been a columnist for *The Guardian*, The Forward, Moment, *MSNBC* and *Rolling Stone*, and a contributor to *The New Yorker* and *The Atlantic*. He is a former senior fellow at the Center for American Progress and the World Policy Institute.

EA: I was one of the first people to use fascism with regard to the Trump presidency, because it doesn't look like Hitler really at all.

It looks a little bit like Mussolini. But it came to me one day that American fascism would look American, rather than European. The first week of Trump's presidency, he kept responding to everything as if it were about him.

I had not paid that much attention to Trump. I'd never watched an episode of *The Apprentice*. I knew him as an annoyance in the gossip pages, basically. But I turned to my then partner, and I said, he just doesn't understand the job. There's a way to act like you are president and Trump hasn't figured that out yet.

But he never changed. Everything remained completely about him. And the destruction of all forms of opposition and criticism, to the degree that one can get away with it, in order to preserve one man rule is a pretty good definition of fascism. I read Jason Stanley's book, which came out very early in the Trump administration, and I thought he made a very good case that there was a lot of parallels historically speaking, between Trump and how we define fascism as scholars. Stanley's book put me on sort of firm ground on this feeling I had, that Trump was doing his best to bring fascism gradually to the United States, and if he had a second term, he would have succeeded. Towards the end he got a little desperate and it became more obvious.

> *The destruction of all forms of opposition and criticism, to the degree that one can get away with it, in order to preserve one man rule is a pretty good definition of fascism.*

BG: *Do you think American politics has always had a fascistic strain?*

EA: There's a very large constituency for fascism in the Republican Party. When we first knew each other, I thought I cannot believe these Republicans. And yet, I had no idea. I underestimated them, completely. I never thought we'd be where we are. Sad.

America's always had a very, very strong commitment to white supremacy. And there have been a lot of people at the top very uncomfortable with democracy if it doesn't go their way. Like democracy is only allowed to operate so long as it's within the boundaries and it's respecting the power of people who have power. So those are two elements that could evolve into fascism. But I wouldn't say that they were necessarily fascist. If you were a black person living in the South, up until the 1960s, you were living under an apartheid regime. You were living without rights. It's not quite the same thing as living in an autocracy. I'm not sure that I would say it's fascism. I think fascism has certain qualities that were lacking until Trump came in. The fascist we used to talk about was Huey Long. Because it was all about him. I think you need that element. And maybe there were some elements of it in George Wallace, but I don't think it makes sense to talk about American fascism before Trump.

> *It came to me one day that American fascism*
> *would look American, rather than European…*
> *And the destruction of all forms of opposition*
> *and criticism in order to preserve one man*
> *rule is a pretty good definition of fascism.*

BG: *You wrote a book called* The Cause: The Fight for American Liberalism from Franklin Roosevelt to Barack Obama. *To paraphrase Country Joe, what are we fighting for when we fight for America's liberal traditions?*

EA: The problem with liberalism is that it's boring. It's complicated and boring, two terrible things, in terms of politics. But what we're really fighting for is process, we're fighting for people to have the right to get what they're promised and, if they're not getting what they're promised, to have some process by which they can peaceably use the law to get it. Either by combining through unions, or having fair courts, or voting the proper politicians that they support. So the process itself has to be protected. And that's what Trump and his people have gone after. They understand that—they couldn't explain it, but they understand it. So liberalism has to defend boring stuff. And, now that I think about it, the Supreme Court has brought us closer to fascism, because the people Trump has appointed are successfully undermining that ability to follow the law and get a fair hearing.

BG: *I want you to react to a quote from that book. You write, 'FDR would personally chase the plutocrats from the temple of democracy'. You quote him saying, 'Let us be frank in acknowledgement of the truth. That many amongst us have made obeisance to mammon, that the prophets of speculation, the easy road without toil, have lured us from the old barricades'. Why do you think American Christians kind of miss that one? Why are they not out in mass attacking leaders and businesses and policies that, to use Roosevelt's term, have paid obeisance to mammon? They sort of don't care about that part.*

EA: I think people care about their own individual wellbeing. And in America they have overly optimistic hopes of achieving a betterment of their wellbeing because of the myth of the American dream. I don't think democracy itself is that attractive to people. The idea of it, I don't think it's that meaningful. They think of themselves as living in a democracy, but they're much more interested in their own individual autonomy. The American movies, as opposed to other countries' movies, are much more about one man, sometimes a woman, standing up against the crowd and succeeding on his or her own. This American individualism makes it hard for people to join together to see their collective interest. And the idea that they can achieve what they want to achieve in this economy and this political culture is deeply ingrained in people.

In every aspect of their political culture: the music, the movies, the gossip, newspapers, the political coverage. And one reason Trump succeeded… it's kind of crazy because his personality, in my view, to any sane person, is incredibly unattractive. But the idea that he made this all about him and his personality, that's consistent with how people see politics. It's just about which guy you like better. Not what he's gonna do.

BG: *After all these years, does his continued popularity, after all the shit that he's pulled, in a country with supposedly strong liberal traditions, surprise you at this point?*

EA: I asked a big question about America. How is it that 74 million people could have voted for this guy? Who are these people?

I live a very rarefied life. I live on the Upper West Side of Manhattan. I vacation in nice places. I had a doctor once, who I've stayed friends with, went to high school with him. He might have voted for Trump, he won't say. He's the only person that I know, that I've met in this entire eight-year period that might have voted for Trump. Everyone I know is horrified and disgusted by Trump. So I don't know this country where Trump could be president. It's a mystery to me. And I don't really want to know it, it's horrible. But that's really the question. Donald Trump is a symptom, not a cause. And he's a symptom of something very sick in America, and it's a very large portion of Americans. It's like, at least a third of Americans. And that says something terrible about our country, but also something very interesting.

I feel like those people, they hate me. They hate liberal Jewish intellectuals from New York. They feel that people like me have contempt for them. And they want to take out their resentment on people like me, who support Democrats and think that they have no education, and their lives suck, and who would want to live wherever the hell they live. And they're not entirely wrong, the cultural gap is enormous in this country. And people like me want nothing to do with people like them. And they know it. And even though the *New York Times* is always sucking up to these people, it's a suck up of condescension. They want to blame their situation, even though they get much more back from the federal government than they pay in taxes, and the country is set up so they have two senators for 300,000 people, whereas we have two senators for 20 million people or 40 million people. Even though the country is set up for their benefit, they feel this enormous sense of resentment over the fact that they believe themselves not to be treated with respect by the, quote-unquote, coastal elite.

And they are not treated with respect by the coastal elite in part because they support politicians like Donald Trump, because they're so easy to fool. Because they blame immigrants for their situation, rather than their refusal to invest in education and industries that have a future. It's a bad situation. The Republicans have always in my lifetime exploited this resentment. But Trump, he's so nakedly hypocritical and distasteful. He's a rapist. He's a criminal. He's a con man. He speaks in nonsense all the time. I mean, it's so pathetic. I feel like in Europe, they have a much higher class of fascists than we do.

> *Because they blame immigrants for their situation, rather than their refusal to invest in education and industries that have a future.*

BG: *Explain, as an expert on propaganda and media, how does a country, known for its higher institutions of learning, leadership in science and technology, free press, have a political party whose members believe an election was stolen in large numbers when there's no evidence to support it? The Republican running an insurance office in La Crosse, Wisconsin, when someone brings him a claim, he asks them for proof. You said your car was hit. Bring it in or there's no claim. How can most Republicans still believe that the election was stolen?*

EA: They didn't believe it to begin with. They only believed it after it was repeated over and over and over by Trump and by Fox News and by all the other mini–Fox News and the Republican Party. They've just heard it over and over and they've just accepted it.

One deep thought I've had since I became a historian is that we're really two countries that have never matched. One country landed in New England, and one country landed in Virginia. And the people who landed in New England, the people who moved from England to New England, made the best decision that any group of people has ever made in history. They automatically became the healthiest, best educated, and collectively wealthiest people there ever have been, up till that point in history. Whereas the people in Virginia, they live a miserable life, first terrified that they would be killed by their slaves or by the local Indians. And a lot of them were sent there because they had no choice. They would send one guy to run the place, and everybody else would either be a criminal or someone working there for a brief period to get enough money to go back home immediately. And they developed in two entirely different cultures. Obviously, one is a slave culture, and one was an anti-slave culture. And the Confederacy had a set of values that were rooted in the past, rooted in white supremacy, rooted in misogyny. And rooted in fear.

New England had a much more optimistic way of doing things. You had the very first university founded, it was Harvard in I think the 1630s. And these two countries, these two cultures have never fully meshed, they're still very different. You can find pockets of New England in Nashville or Austin or Asheville. But basically, it's two separate countries. You can see it most clearly with abortion laws today. They've been living this way forever on that side of the divide. Trump said a lot of things when he was running in 2016 that he would never say today because he's accommodated himself to the views of the Confederacy. He didn't believe them at first, he's become this right wing nut in order to appeal to these people, because that's what they demand of their leaders. And that's what he cares about. I think I live in a relatively decent country, but it's a different country than half the country lives in.

> *I feel like in Europe, they have a much higher class of fascists than we do.*

BG: *How would a second Trump presidency differ from the first?*

EA: I always answer this question saying I'm a historian, I don't predict the future. But I would point out that all the people who acted as human guardrails are gone. And the courts are no longer dependable. And a lot of the things Trump was doing were consistent with a violent fascist regime. And so we're going to have many more elements of fascism. And I don't know if democracy can survive it, I don't know. Nobody knows that.

BG: *I'm in Budapest and you've referred to Viktor Orbán in your writing. I just had dinner with an official from Orbán's government, very erudite, charming guy and gave a lot of heartfelt, direct answers, I was impressed with his willingness to engage. What's your view of Viktor Orbán and why are American conservatives so absolutely in love with this guy?*

EA: American conservatives know that they're a minority and they can't win an election in a democratic country. So, Orbán, like Putin, appears to have legitimized illiberalism and anti-democratic actions in order to remain in power. And they're like, whoa, you can do this. That's awesome.

BG: *To have the CPAC (Conservative Political Action Committee) convention in Budapest was pretty extraordinary.*

EA: I know. But the good thing about the MAGA people is that they're not hiding anything. I would say if America reelected Trump, it would be getting what it deserves. But, see, it's not fair. Because it's not America, it's part of America. As I said, it would mean that one side of the culture defeated the other side of the culture. And that side will have to suffer underneath the boot of the first one. I'll be fine, I suppose. But a lot of people who need protection won't get it. And that's what's really frightening about the future.

BG: *I interviewed a Serbian journalist years ago, liberal guy, and he made a comment that Eastern Europeans love strongmen. Do you think there's something in human nature that makes us attracted to strongmen or authoritarian leaders?*

EA: People like order, I like order. You live in a place that's anarchic, it's hard to relax. It's hard to feel comfortable. If you're living in what you consider to be disorder, then the idea of a strongman who promises he can maintain order is very attractive, it would be to anyone. And what the right has been selling to its constituency is the idea of disorder in the United States, that black people and immigrants are coming to kill you and rape your daughters and so forth. And New York is impossible, you can't walk around in New York, you're going to get killed. It's complete nonsense. But it's created this fear among people that leads them to say, we need a strongman too. And they've also created a certain metaphorical position for the United States in the world, everybody's taking advantage of us, China's kicking our ass, and Mexicans are sending us their criminals. And so they respond by saying, well, democracy is nice, but we need a strongman. And that's just normal. People do that in wartime all the time. It'd be nice to have democracy, but we've got to win this war. And what they're creating is sort of a permanent war footing against immigrants, and trans people, etcetera. People who they've come to feel that they are under siege, thanks in part to Rupert Murdoch and other nefarious figures who exploit them for profit.

> *People like order, I like order. You live*
> *in a place that's anarchic, it's hard to*
> *relax. It's hard to feel comfortable.*
>
> *If you're living in what you consider to be disorder,*
> *then the idea of a strongman who promises*
> *he can maintain order is very attractive.*

BG: *What's a modern Eric Alterman people oriented liberal vision for a better future?*

EA: Werner Sombart wrote an essay (in 1996) called, 'Why there is no socialism in the United States'. The most important reason is that the people who run the United States have always tried to divide and rule. In that period, it was Germans versus Italians versus Jews versus Irish versus blacks. And today, more than anything, it's race that divides us. And the exploitation of race. If people could see their common interest, they'd have a lot more power than they do. It's a terrible thing to say, if it weren't for this Dobbs decision, Trump would probably win. And the reason the Dobbs decision is important is because it shows people who care about reproductive freedom that they have to get involved in politics. They can't just expect to get what they want without playing the game.

Liberalism has suffered because people have not seen the need to fight for the things they want. They got it through the courts since the 1960s. And rich people have kind of opted out. If you look at Project 2025, everyone has an interest in preventing that. But people have to stop dividing themselves, they have to stop saying, 'I don't agree with you about Zionism, so I can't work with you'. Or, 'I think you're insensitive about how you talk about race, or you're not using the right pronouns', etcetera, and put what's important up front.

I told this story when I used to lecture around the country about Ralph Reed and Newt Gingrich. You can have this story, it's a good one. Newt Gingrich went to Ralph Reed when Reed was head of the Christian Coalition, and he said, here's my Contract for America, I want to take out a full-page ad in every issue of *TV Guide* and *Reader's Digest,* which at that time were the two highest circulation magazines in America. And I want you to pay for it, Ralph. And Ralph looked at the Contract for America and said, it's funny that you would say that Newt, because none of my issues are in here. This is all economic stuff and political stuff. There's nothing about Jesus or anything. And Newt said, Ralph, wouldn't you rather be having this conversation with the Speaker of the House? Let's argue about it after we've won.

And liberals have never been able to do that, they've never been able to settle their differences in order to win. And then decide how to go about dealing with them. So my wish as a liberal is that people could see that the way to pursue their interests is not to divide themselves but to multiply themselves by having coalitions on what they agree on, rather than fighting over the narcissism of small differences. It's not that brilliant a vision.

Here's hoping. That's all we can do. Well, could do more, but ultimately, it's all we can do.

CHAPTER 8

ROMANIA

Ceausescu and Coming to America

Whereupon I tour Bucharest's Museum of Communism with a Romanian publishing couple… visit the synagogue-based Jewish Museum and Romania's Holocaust Museum to learn how the country's 800,000 Jewish population was reduced to 8,000… discover by accident the hometown of my great grandfather then take a morning train to the Danube to walk the streets he walked before coming to America… and begin the final journey to Istanbul.

A brief history of Romania's turbulent century of authoritarian monarchy, fascism, communist dictatorship, and Christian nationalism.

1927: Corneliu Zelea Codreanu founds the Legion of the Archangel Michael, later known as the Iron Guard. The organization combines elements of nationalism, fascism, and Orthodox Christianity, promoting a vision of Romania as a nation under threat from Jews, communists, and other perceived enemies.

1930: The Iron Guard gains popularity, particularly among youth and rural communities. The organization engages in violent acts against political opponents and Jews.

1933: Prime Minister Ion G. Duca bans the Iron Guard. Codreanu and other leaders are arrested, and the group is forced underground.

1934-1938: Despite the ban, the Iron Guard grows in influence and, in 1937, becomes the third-largest party in the Romanian parliament.

1938: King Carol II establishes a royal dictatorship and takes steps to suppress the Iron Guard, including the arrest and execution of Codreanu and other leaders.

1940: Amidst ongoing political instability, King Carol II abdicates. General Ion Antonescu forms a coalition government with the Iron Guard, named the National Legionary State. The regime aligns Romania with Nazi Germany and implements anti-Semitic policies.

1941: The Iron Guard stages a rebellion against Antonescu's government. It is crushed, and Antonescu dissolves the Iron Guard, imprisoning or executing many of its members.

1941-1944: Romania remains an ally of Nazi Germany under Antonescu's rule, participating in the invasion of the Soviet Union and the deportation and mass murder of Jews.

1945: With the defeat of Nazi Germany, Romania falls under Soviet influence, and the communist regime suppresses all fascist and nationalist organizations, including the remnants of the Iron Guard.

———

As I settle into my Bucharest hotel, I wonder at the interior lives of my Romanian ancestors who fled persecution and deprivation to come to America around the turn of the 20th century. All of my aunts and uncles have passed away, as did my parents a long time ago, and no one seems quite sure of my grandma Yetta's Romanian birthplace.

Twelve years ago, a distant cousin from my grandmother's side contacted me and shared the family's genealogy. We met with other cousins in Los Angeles. Names that I had not heard for decades—that uncle, that great aunt, that distant cousin— were shared with updates and remembrances. We exchanged an occasional email or two after that but nothing more.

I do an email search and rediscover her notes. And a note from another cousin sharing a short history from an uncle.

My great grandfather's name was Solomon Rothenberg. It strikes me for the first time that my father Sol (he was always called Sol or Solly, never Solomon) was named after him. The note went on to say he had a great voice, a cantor (one who leads a Jewish congregation in song and prayer) in Romania and America. I remember now. The old Brooklyn synagogue where I was bar mitzvah'd had been the scene of his cantor work, though he passed well before I was born. The note then shares vital details. He sold fish in a town along the Danube River. Galați, (pronounced Galatz). Some said he built his fish selling business into a suc- cessful entrepreneurial concern. Others said he did the fishing himself. No matter. Sol sold fish. On the Danube.

I look up the train schedule. There is a four-hour train to Galați departing 8am, returning same time the next day. Eurail ordering is dysfunctional in Romania so I go to the Bucharest Nord station to buy my ticket for Monday, two days from now. Neither ticket agent speaks English. My reaction is the same as it has been in other commercial situations on this trip: 1) It's their country and I should know their language so I best power through it, and 2) It seems a commercial opportunity that the major train hub of the country might be able to serve international customers. I go to ticket machine and buy it there. It takes a minute to navigate but, voila, my return ticket to Galați pops out of the machine.

Located in Bucharest's Old Town, the Museum of Communism explores daily life under the post-WWII Marxist-Leninist regime with a focus on the brutal years of Ceausescu's personality cult. I meet longtime Romanian publishing colleague Alexandru Oprescu and his wife Georgiana nearby.

ALEXANDRU OPRESCU
Looking to America

Born in a small town near Craiova, Alex has a bachelor's degree in English Literature and a Masters in Anglo-American studies from the University of Craiova. He has published literary articles in the Romanian cultural magazine *Scrisul Romanesc*, along with translating several novels and poetry books, including former NPR on-air personality Andrei Codrescu's The Art of Forgetting.

While touring the museum, we meet Radu, a museum tour guide and history student, who takes us through the exhibits.

R: There is a history room with exhibits on how communism took power. Social policies during the early years and repression on this wall. Next is on Nicolae Ceausescu with exhibits on education, life in the military, industry. And lastly, we have set up a living room and a kitchen, extravagant, for the well-connected and higher ups lived, as opposed to austere for the average Romanian.

BG: *Was there an ideological justification for that? Or they just like to live well?*

R: Within the ideological bounds of communism, you cannot justify a higher living standard than your peers, right? No matter your job, no matter your perceived status, because in such a society, there are no differences in status. There was no justification to this. It was just people who have the means, who have the connections, this is their opportunity. This is what happened in Romania, and all across the Eastern Bloc. Russia hasn't recovered, the oligarchs still dominate the economy. In Romania, our local oligarchs, local barons, these people have enough money to influence local elections, they still have enough contacts in government and administration to make sure things go their way. They're very difficult to challenge and they're not in front, they're just in the shadows, somewhere behind propping up one candidate or another. Directing one institution or the other for their friends.

BG: *For you, what's the purpose and the importance of this museum?*

R: I'm a history student, I think it's very important that it exists. People come and ask me, is this a communist or an anti-communist museum? A museum presents the bad and the good and lets you decide. What's unfortunate is that this museum like so many others about communism in Romania are private. The state doesn't really like to sponsor museums about communism.

AO: We talked about this. They don't like it because some of the old communists are still in power. They would be exposing themselves.

R: And educating the population to what happened. Now it's more convenient to have a lot of people live with the false sense that they were more prosperous back then. And things were better. That Ceausescu gave them jobs and apartments and so forth. This museum is especially for younger Romanians. Because the older generations, they're very full of themselves. 'I've heard the rhetoric, oh, I lived through it, I don't need to go to a museum.' Here we actually understand the process. But for the youth, the people who have no idea what it was like during communism, who maybe put up with all sorts of stories, some good, some bad, this should be the place to come to in order to get this general picture.

BG: *How healthy of a democracy does Romania have today?*

R: We're not a very healthy democracy. The root cause starts, when the revolution came, a group of former communists seized power, they grouped themselves into the so-called National Salvation Front. And they promised to be an extraordinary form of government until elections can be organized. And then they'll just dissolve themselves and go peacefully away.

BG: *Sounds great.*

R: Yeah, until they decided to run the elections as a political party. Obviously, you can guess who won the elections. So you have the former communists now back in power.

So that's actually the reason, not just inertia from being stuck in communism for so long, it's also the fact that now you have so many opportunities you can tap into, you can just be a parasite on a state company. You can steal as much as possible, start your own company, bankrupt the former company, like one of our neighbors did, he used to work for an elevator maintenance company.

BG: *Is there a general Romanian attitude towards American elections or American politics?*

R: That's an interesting question. The United States is most definitely a model. Ever since the First World War ended, the United States was this beacon of prosperity, democratic stability, that Romanians look to. France was still our main model. After the war, there was this belief that the Americans are going to come and invade the Warsaw Pact, and free us all from Communism, which is something that persisted. We had the slogan, *Vin americanii*, the Americans are coming. That lasted well into the 60s. And during communism, as well, American society was something to be admired. They had the jeans, they were cool, later they had Walkmans. That's where all the good products were coming from. They had Pepsi, they had Coke, we only had Pepsi. And the U.S. with this whole land of prosperity and opportunity thing kind of appealed a lot to Romanians who were just out of communism, out of the dictatorship, looking to carve a path for life for themselves. And it also helped that we got a lot of American movies coming in, American music. Products came a bit later. Nowadays, the American dream is still something that lives in Romanians' hearts, the idea that over there, you can go and you can become someone from nothing. This is very appealing. Trump appeals to some Romanians because of that harder, authoritarian, conservative line that they also saw in Ceausescu.

We also have Romanians admiring Ion Antonescu, a general and dictator of Romania during the Second World War. He also has a kind of a cult, although after he was declared a war criminal, things have loosened in that direction.

BG: *If the U.S. did become authoritarian, would that be a disappointment and a concern for people in countries like yours?*

R: That would probably be a very serious blow to the belief in liberalism, the faith that democracy can work, that democracy is a system that is worth its while. It pays to defend democracy. It pays to have a government elected by the people, for the people, and not just one person on top calling all the shots. If the United States did go that route, I'm afraid it might be a blow, because there isn't any other democratic model in the world quite as popular, and quite as universal as the United States. Probably many countries go to, when you think democracy and freedom, you probably associate it with the United States.

Democracy in Romania does not have a very good track record. Because when it came over here, the people who seized power during the revolution gave former communists and former secret police officials the means and the opportunities to steal from the state. And so nowadays, you do hear, it's frustrating, democracy and capitalism. We're told the economy's booming, and we're about to overtake Poland, and that it has tripled since the fall of communism, which may be perfectly true on paper, but you don't feel it in your pocket, you know? This is a never-ending source of frustration. And yeah, again, this feeds into the whole, what is capitalism, what is democracy? And you also hear, speaking of democracy, when Ceausescu said, I want a Metro in Bucharest, there was a Metro built. And when Ceausescu said, I want a highway, there was a highway built. And now look, these people can't build a Metro in 10 years, true and very sad. But like I keep telling people who I hear this rhetoric from, we must have faith. At some point, things are probably going to be better, you're going to have the old elite die out. We see all the examples of these rich kids just blowing their parents' wealth on nothing. So we need to be hopeful that things are going to change, you need to have patience. I think the same goes for the United States.

———

The next day, I join Alex and Georgiana for lunch.

BG: *As a Romanian, why does the American election and American politics matter to you?*

AO: Romania has a great tradition of looking up to America, especially for its values, for freedom, for liberty. As an up-and-coming country with the same aspirations, everyone looks towards

America to be the shining beacon that shows the way. Romanians recognize the same rhetoric that we had in the communist period. A populist rhetoric, of singing to the same fears, the universal fears about jobs and security. As Radu was saying, some people like this, because they remember the fondness they had about the communist regime, seeing so much division and illiberal discourse.

BG: *When I looked into my own genealogy, my great grandfather saw economic opportunity. But from what I hear from you, in terms of history of Romanians' interest in America, they also saw a culture that was free from the repressive political ideologies that have characterized Romania in the last century or two.*

AO: Oh, sure, Romanians went abroad for economic prosperity. But when they got there, they got to see something else, a better system, a better way of governance. Most of all, I think they saw opportunity, maybe what would later become 'the American dream'. Opportunity was something very scarce in most parts of the world.

BG: *There are some people who are cynical about America being a beacon of anything because of its treatment of Native Americans and African slaves and refugees. What do you say to them?*

AO: Well, I can agree to the facts. But being practical, let's find another country that overall does it better. We don't have one of consequence. Because you can be a small country like Sweden or Finland and be extremely social oriented and do extraordinary things. But they don't have a consequence on the world stage. They cannot influence other countries like America does. Another thing to appreciate looking at America is that they somewhat learned from their mistakes. They try to learn, they try to change, they try to adapt.

BG: *What was your reaction to Viktor Orbán going to Kyiv and then to visit Trump and Putin?*

AO: Romania has experience with Orbán, as we talked about Tuşnad, and his connection with the Hungarian minority in Romania, which is the largest one. So we know his tendencies of stirring things up. He thinks he can gain something from it, but I'm not sure what he's gonna gain in the end by having this position towards Ukraine and towards Russia. What can Russia do for him really? Because of all the historical background, Hungary constantly—and falsely—lays claim to Transylvania, and this is why Romania is always on its toes about the Orbán regime.

Russia tries in Moldova to slow the reforms. Orbán is doing it in the European Union and tries to cut help for Ukraine and be a voice for Putin in the European Parliament. He looks like a very bellicose leader. And I think he identifies with Putin, in that he wants sort of the same regime in Hungary. He cracked down on the press in Hungary. It is a democratic country, but it has its issues.

BG: *You seemed to have strong feelings when we saw the museum display about Ceausescu's ban of abortions and contraception, that something similar is happening in the United States.*

AO: I am a product of that decree of the banned abortions. I have one brother and one sister who are much older, 14 and 17 years older than me. I was sort of a mistake that came into the family, now a happy mistake. And if it wasn't for that abortion decree, I wouldn't be here. But Romania was full of orphanages of unwanted children. Romania had an extremely high rate of deaths because women were trying to make clandestine abortions. And if they caught you, you would go to prison. It was an extreme terror against the population that was closely regulated through state mandated gynecologists that would check the women working in factories, like they were cattle. They put terror in one of the more pleasurable and free activities in life.

Pickled peppers and cucumbers are served.

BG: *My grandfather loved those.*

AO: They are a staple dish here. So we know the history firsthand. We know the history from our grandmothers, we know the history from our mothers. They know exactly what would happen. So we were shocked, actually, that in the U.S. something like this would happen.

—

Alex and Georgiana give me an insider's tour of the city. The National History Museum of Romania along with nearby monuments and historic buildings. The Carturesti Carusel bookstore, a modern, multi-floored emporium of brightly presented books, vinyl records, DVDs, wines, and accessories, with loads of kids wandering the aisles with parents and friends. I watch them from the top floor café and recall Bill of Rights author James Madison's admonition for sustaining a democracy: 'Popular Government, without popular information, or the means of acquiring it, is but a Prologue to a Farce or a Tragedy; or, perhaps, both.' Put in modern terms, well-trafficked bookstores and libraries, well-funded public schools and universities, and an assertive, unfettered free press are essentials of a healthy democracy. Which is why attacks on teachers and colleges and journalists and authors are the predictable political vomit of fascist-minded leaders and agitators.

Romania moves me. Family memories are triggered in the act of ordering pickled peppers and cucumbers. My father loved them because his Romanian ancestors loved them.

At the entrance to the Jewish Museum, I meet Paul, who acts as informal guide and Jewish historian. I tell him that I am here to look for scenes from my great grandfather's life. This Bucharest synagogue is not the scale of Budapest's Doheny Street, but it's an experience akin to Peniche or Barcelona's civil war sites or Dachau's ghastly corridors. I feel the presence of the thousands of Jews who passed through here. Solomon and Yetta were certainly here. Train travel by that time was affordable and widely used. I wander past the seats, run my hand over pews and walls and doors that might have been warmed by my ancestors. It's a marvelous and familiar feeling. And, wistful, as I want to experience what a service might have been like in 1890.

Paul tells me to lower my expectations for Galați—not even enough for a minyan (a 10-person prayer group) there. I assure Paul that it's OK. It's quite enough for me to walk the streets my great grandfather walked and watch the Danube tributaries that he contemplated 150 years ago.

The next morning, I'm off to Galați. I buy some suspicious looking hot takeaway treats at the train station. And water. We are scheduled to arrive just past noon.

The train is old but comfortable. I'm told to have modest expectations of arrival times and amenities. A woman has my seat. She has several bags with her. She smiles to confirm that she isn't moving and, anyway, the train is empty, but I let her know if the train fills, I'm coming back for her. Eventually, it does. Should I kick an old lady out of her train seat? Sure!

During the journey, I take photos and videos of the passing hills and farms and small shops. It's a beautiful country. I hope to come back.

Galați is the terminal stop so I don't have to calculate my move to my bags and the exit as carefully as I have through the trip. A brief lapse in attention—and I've had those often as I mused about the next interview or city—and suddenly you crane your neck and realize you are at your stop and your bags are… somewhere… and you have 30 seconds to figure it out and get off the train.

I step onto the platform and look up at the electronic arrival and departure monitor. The next train is to Iași, the other Yiddish center of Jewish life, up the river, and the declared birthplace of my great uncle Louis on his passport. This corridor was a major center of European Jewish life. The number sticks in my head. 800,000 Jews. Down to 8,000. The birthplace by many accounts of Yiddish theater which spawned New York Jewish theater which informed New York standup comedy and the Catskills and a large swath of the American entertainment industry. Antisemitic conspiracy theories harangue Jewish bankers as the cabal controlling the world. Jews only got into finance because the handling of money was considered unclean, filthy in Christian and Muslim societies. And since Jews were subhuman, they were given control of finance and lending and, well, they got good at it. They were forbidden from owning land in most of Europe and barred from many guilds and professions. And when they tried to join the fray in New York theater, they were shut out. So many moved to Los Angeles and founded their own studios in the emerging filmed entertainment business.

In my month in Kabul for *WAR: The Afterparty*, I was verbally assaulted by an Islamist in a swimming pool. 'America is controlled by Zionists', he told me. I asked him what he thought of Jews. He was flummoxed, then went into a Dari diatribe, interpreted by his skinny young pal, about how Jews control the banks and the media. I answered, "Yeah, and comedy too."

And it started here.

In the late nineteenth century, Jewish theater troupes were founded in several Romanian cities. Yiddish theater is widely believed to have been founded by poet and playwright Abraham Goldfaden (1840–1908). Goldfaden met troubadour Israel Grodner of Berl Broder's traveling singing troupe in 1876 in Iași, where they founded the first Yiddish theater company. The first newspaper reference to a Jewish theater in Romania was in a review by Mihai Eminescu in *Curierul de Iași* in 1876, in which he described a troupe of 16 Jewish actors, including tavern singers and cantors, who performed in Iași wine cellars under Goldfaden's management.

My aunt Ruth, daughter of Grandma Yetta, performed in Yiddish theater in New York as a young woman. With (Yiddish theater icon, then popular television actor) Fyvush Finkel, she declared, if you forgot that bit of data from previous conversations. When she was a little girl, a few years old, I was told she got lost on a very crowded Coney Island Beach. My uncle Abe was supposed to be watching her. Sam and Yetta were beside themselves with worry. After a feverish search, they discovered little Ruth performing for the police officers at the beach station, not a care in the world. Performing, the act of delighting other people, was an essential part of the culture. My daughter Andrea once posited that my father Sol loved driving a cab in New York so he could entertain people with his jokes and stories over and over again all day long.

Galați is a port town on the Danube River and the eighth largest city in Romania. I get a ride to the hotel, the room overlooking the Danube. I'm hungry but tired and struggle to decide whether to rest or dine. I am told at the front desk that there are plenty of restaurants in city center, a 10–20-minute walk away. In that direction is the Galați synagogue.

The largely urban Jewish population in Romania increased significantly in the middle of the 19th century. There was already a long history of racist persecution, with authorities deciding in 1650 and 1741 that Jews had to wear clothing revealing their ethnicity. The Jews of Târgu Neamț experienced the first blood libel in 1710, charged with killing a Christian child for ritual purposes. Antisemitic conspiracy theories have long justified brutal attacks, from the Russian *Protocols of the Elders of Zion,* distributed widely by automaker Henry Ford, to Hitler's rants against Jewish freemasons. Modern-day Qanon conspiracy memes still rail against Jewish bankers (who control only one percent of the world's wealth), not just in the U.S., but all over the world. On my Thai island home, a German musician attacked me for being a freemason and a Trump-supporting Canadian seller of new age botanicals told people I was illuminati, two centuries-old Jewish blood libel conspiracies. Qanon insists liberals drink the adrenochrome of Christian children, thus, elect Donald Trump who will break up the Satanic cabal.

In October of 1940, the Iron Guard tortured and beat Jews in the streets, while looting their shops. After Romania entered WWII on the side of the Nazis at the start of Operation Barbarossa, atrocities against Jews were routine, starting with an Iaşi pogrom. A Wiesel Commission report released by the Romanian government in 2004 estimates between 280,000 and 380,000 Jews were murdered in Romania during the war, along with another 135,000 deaths and deportations to concentration camps in Northern Transylvania, under Hungarian control.

During the Ceausescu regime, there was further religious persecution, resulting in a mass emigration to Israel, with Jews sold at $4,000 – $6,000 per head as bounties by the government. Jews were expected to take part in the Ceausescu personality cult in order to avoid interrogation rooms, forced labor, or social ostracization. They were sometimes imprisoned to force emigration and a large payment to the regime.

The Galaţi synagogue is a short walk from the hotel. I stop to admire the Danube and an old church building nearby, then walk to the city center. The promenade along the river is a favorite of families and lovers and kids. There is a massive propellor monument, presumably a tribute to the vital place of Danube shipping to the town. Close by is a statue of Ion Brătianu, a bearded, stern-looking fellow in waistcoat with left hand in his trouser pocket, pointing out to the Danube. In 1875, under his premiership, Jews were forbidden to settle in the countryside. My great grandfather no doubt experienced Mister Brătianu's various persecutions.

It's now pushing 2pm and I'm hungry and seek something approximating local cuisine but restaurants are either closed or serving western style pizza, burgers, or sandwiches. I decide to stop by what looks like a Jewish center on my map app but it's an office complex. I decide to wait a little longer for lunch and walk on to the synagogue.

As expected, it is chained shut. No contact information on the exterior or on the web. It does not look well-trafficked. All I can do is inspect the fading star of David on the fence, the nondescript exterior, and imagine Solomon Rothenberg's grand voice singing Hebrew passages written by the ancients. I run my hand along the building's exterior and imagine him holding little Yetta's hand down this alley.

When I walk down a street in Manhattan, I know that my father drove his taxi there during his quarter century in the profession. He started with a Checker cab then had a yellow Dodge, medallion 6C48. So I talk to him, imagine who was in his cab, what back street diner he was choosing for a meal. I feel his presence. And so, for Solomon Rothenberg, the best I can do is walk his streets. And imagine why he left the familiarity of his homeland for the United States.

After talking to Alex and Paul and Radu and recalling the political conversations of my parents and aunts and uncles, I can guess. He was tired of being under the thumb of brutalist autocrats. Disgusted with roving bands of racist thugs in the streets. Outraged at attacks on artists and educators and people thinking differently. Sick of watching hoarders of wealth and power insist on their privilege for more wealth and power, sucking the working man and woman dry. Appalled at the use of political violence to oppress and intimidate the masses. Offended at the crass vulgarity of men who consider themselves to be ordained by God, to be above the rule of law, beyond the reach of justice.

Me too, Solly.

After enjoying a traditional Romanian dinner in an outdoor bistro, I visit the British rock and roll-themed riverfront bar next to my hotel for a final sampling of Romanian palinkas. I rise early the next morning to begin my long journey home via my last stop at Istanbul's Bosporus Strait. There is a train leaving the Galați station for Iași. I consider boarding it for a moment but there's just no time. I think how I might say goodbye to Solomon and Yetta and Jacob and Paul and the other distant relatives that once graced this station platform, staring out at the same scene, excited to travel someplace new or familiar.

I calculate the remaining moments before departure. I look up the Jewish prayer for the dead on my phone and, in perhaps the only Hebrew spoken here for a long while, I recite the Kaddish for those who came before me. For Solomon and Jenny and Rachel and Yetta and my parents Sol and Claire and brother Jeffrey and everyone on the list of names sent me by my cousin 10 years back. A prayer in remembrance of the dead, for those who gave me life, for those who nurtured me through childhood, for those whose artistry and joy and love of life infused my upbringing and way of experiencing the world.

> *Yis'ga'dal v'yis'kadash sh'may ra'bbo, b'olmo dee'vro chir'usay v'yamlich malchu'say, b'chayaychon uv'yomay'chon uv'chayay d'chol bais Yisroel, ba'agolo u'viz'man koriv; v'imru Omein.*

CHAPTER 9

TURKEY

Erdogan and the Journey's End

Whereupon I complete my traversing of the European continent by crossing the Bosporus Strait… meet a tattooist who offers free Atatürk tats each year… am helped through a Turkish menu by a woman who describes life under Erdogan in vivid detail… then hear Bella Ciao *performed live as I get out of a taxi in front of my hotel and join in for the very last stanza.*

Before crossing the Bosporus Strait, I visit Istanbul's Atatürk Museum, housing the personal clothing, collections, historical documents, photographs and paintings of Mustafa Kemal Atatürk, Turkey's first president. On the heels of the Ottoman Empire's defeat in World War One, Atatürk founded the Republic of Turkey, implementing reforms that secularized and westernized the country. Most all the exhibits are in Turkish and it's a brief, mostly impressionistic introduction to his history and impact.

I take the Metro for a meeting with Danny, a tattooist who provides free tattoos of Atatürk's signature in formative moments, part tribute and part protest against the prevailing authorities. I watch the Bosporus Strait below me as the train jumps continents and my long European journey comes to a geographic end.

It's been four weeks since walking Gamboa Beach on the Atlantic coast in Portugal.

I exit the subway station and follow Danny's directions to his studio. After talking about his family history, he shares his unique method of honoring Mustafa Kemal Atatürk.

DANNY GARCIA
An Homage to Atatürk

BG: *You gave free Atatürk tattoos to people during the Gezi Park protest some years ago. Tell me about that protest and what motivated you to want to do that?*

DG: I still have friends who have serious problems because of expressing their opinions, especially online. In the primary school in Turkey, it's normal that we sing the national anthem every morning, like the love for Atatürk is pretty much very normal. I do it every year on the November 10, when he died. I ink his signature.

BG: *Tell me the difference in your mind between Atatürk's vision of governing and Erdogan's vision of governing.*

DG: First of all, Atatürk was for keeping religion out of governing.

BG: *How does Erdogan's use of Islamist ideology affect daily life in Turkey?*

DG: You can buy people easily with that. The Islam style from today, it's like more this Arabic style. And Turkey is not Arabic. It doesn't fit. So that's what the Atatürk style thinking is for.

BG: *But Islamists are gaining more influence here.*

DG: Arabic invasion I call it. Turkey is more Greek than anything else in my opinion. Atatürk came, he dawned the Republic of Turkey. He changed so many things, like stopping the Ottoman Empire stuff, the Sharia law, and he brought the beginning of democracy. Now it only looks like democracy, but I think it's not. It's only used as a power tool. People are uneducated. You can feed them with anything.

BG: *How are things different under Erdogan?*

DG: Pre-Erdogan time, it was freer.

BG: *In what way?*

DG: Now you cannot say anything. Everything is directed with one hand. The different TV stations, all saying the same, because Erdogan bought off everything. People don't have a choice anymore. More than twenty years in power now, definitely too long.

BG: *There were recent local elections where Erdogan's party lost. Is there a viable path to removing Erdogan from power democratically?*

DG: It looked very much like that was on the way, like it was the beginning of the end. I hope it will continue.

BG: *Do you think he would try to stay in power by any means?*

DG: Definitely. His party has lost, he's still like a kind of dictator. I think he wasn't elected the last three elections, somehow a play with the votes.

Until 2003, it was beautiful in Turkey. As a tattoo-er, I could make some good money. People were free, not only economically. It's all going radically downward. We felt that first in 2000. One major economic crisis and it fucking never ended. I had many,

many foreign tattoo artists visiting me from all around the world, USA as well. After the Gezi and the bombings after that, nobody comes. People here, the going is really, really hard.

> *Now you cannot say anything.*
> *Everything is directed with one hand.*

BG: *What happens if someone in Istanbul starts actively speaking out against Erdogan?*

DG: At the Gezi, it was the first time the people are all together as one, but he (Erdogan) really pushed back hard, with military, so the people are pretty afraid because he has many people he could send. They almost treat him like he's God. It's violent.

BG: *Official military people, or police, or militias or thugs who support him?*

DG: Militias also. People undercover. The police.

BG: *So if your next-door neighbor starts writing a blog, starting a podcast, putting out flyers on the street, attacking Erdogan…*

DG: They would investigate him. They would even jail him. Give a comment, somewhere on Instagram, they capture it.

BG: *You know people who have been shut down by him.*

DG: Yes. Shut down. But they left the country as well. Germany or Canada or Montenegro.

BG: *Are the elections fair?*

DG: He controls the system behind the elections.

BG: *What's happened over the last 20 years to people who've run against or opposed him? Have people been killed?*

DG: Definitely not killed.

BG: *But their oxygen in terms of effectively running a campaign is shut off.*

DG: Yeah, sure. I think nobody would do that. The biggest problem is still the economy. Everything is getting more expensive and expensive and expensive and incomes stay the same. People do not earn enough money anymore. You buy a car; you buy one for yourself and three for the country. Any car, four times more expensive than you would buy in the country where it's built.

People say maybe there will be some early elections. We hope for the best. It's very bad. I think people have lost interest in caring about these things and speaking about things. Last two, three years, people are really fed up. Right now, there's a new law that they will catch all the stray dogs and kill them all, just like that. It's crazy. He's always making enemies. People are fed up. And attacking always some people, like homosexuals or whatever. It's pretty much fascism we are running right now, pretty much. It's shit. For example, the Kurdish problem. We have no problem with the Kurdish living under us. Like 10 or 20 years ago, I didn't even know who was Kurdish and who was not. They're all Turkish. There's a lot of crazy, weird stuff. He sold the whole country away.

ASYA
The Flower of Resistance

I leave Danny's shop and head to the Metro for a final night out in Istanbul. It's already past 8, so I decide to stop into a kebab restaurant that offers a range of popular Turkish dishes. The menu has no English translation and I don't recognize much of what I see; I'm hungry and am tempted to order anything at this point. The waiter is not interested in helping. A woman in a green skirt, 40ish, calls out from the next table and asks if I need help. She moves to my table and offers a short primer of the menu offerings. I ask her advice. She suggests lahmacun and adana kebab. She has already dined and so she orders for me with a pair of Turkish soft drinks. The name she gives me is Asya, because, like many people in Turkey, she is scared to speak her mind about the country's politics and prefers to keep her true identity to herself.

I tell her about my trip, the places I've been, the things I've learned. She says she loves to travel but has not done much since COVID as she describes what she considers the dreadful state of the Turkish economy and her own struggle to find new work that suits her. After swapping stories about our backgrounds and Turkish life, we move across the street for a cocktail. I ask her to choose and she orders a pair of vodka lemongrass concoctions. She begins to talk more freely about Turkish politics. I ask, if elections were held and Erdogan lost, would she expect a peaceful transfer of power? She answers, no, that Erdogan would never voluntarily relinquish his position. She describes a state of emergency declared in 2016 which resulted in purges of independent media and detention of tens of thousands. More than 50,000 were arrested and over 160,000 fired from their jobs.

A: Before Erdogan came to power in 2002, he was the head of Istanbul municipalities. Even then, he started with Refah, which is the Islamist party. So he had the background and he definitely had the crowd of Islamist people supporting him. But when he created AKP, he tried to make it like a more democratic Islam, like something more in the center right. More a not super fundamentalist Islam.

BG: *Is Erdogan a fascist?*

A: I personally call them fascist. Super authoritarian government. This is very obvious for the last 15 years. Before that, he still depended on many kinds of players, but I would say after the Gezi protests in 2013, and then '15 and '16, he had more problems. And then changes in legislation made him more powerful, oppressing any kind of journalist, any kind of freedom of speech. People used to be able to criticize. We would have newspapers and media criticizing our presidents. Now there is a big split, half of Turkey just kind of supporting it, calling him the sultan, he's the king, he's the person of God or something like this. It's kind of similar to how people were treating sultans back in the Ottoman Empire, like an extension of God. Like the caliphate. Of course, like any kind of fascism, he creates all the time anti-*whatever*. Like, sometimes we're anti-Israel, anti-U.S., sometimes anti some of the neighboring countries, sometimes anti-Kurdish. He always changes his discourse to get the popular vote. The people who are more educated definitely call him fascist, but not openly. Personally, for example, I would not have this conversation over a phone, because I know that a lot of people around me, like just even writing something on Twitter, or having a call about him and criticizing him, get into trouble for nothing really. I'm not a politically active person here in Turkey, it's not possible. I see that, yeah, my life would be much worse and I might end up in prison.

BG: *What happens if you speak against the government?*

A: Depends where you talk. If you talk among your friends, nothing. Someplace public, then you see all the examples of all the journalists who did that. Some of them are in prison. Some are living in Europe. They cannot come back. The people who can actually talk against Erdogan are now not in Turkey. Because the people who are writing in some of the newspapers, companies are being banned, counselors are being censored constantly. There's only I think two channels that can say anything against him. And they have to be very careful and smart, not talking directly against him. Someone would sue you for talking against the president.

Her demeanor has changed. And it's not the vodka lemongrass cocktails. She is releasing years of steam, to a stranger interested in her story. Her eyes begin to tear. The hopelessness, the endless anxiety, the fury at the repression and corruption, at the sheer stupidity—in her view—of incompetent governance. She can't travel freely because of restrictions on Turkish visas, another outcome in her view of an Erdogan misfire. She laughs uneasily about the fact that people don't speak much English as she refers to my menu mishap, then adds that it's something beyond that. In Turkey, she says, education is not a priority. The school system is in decline, by design, in her view. Both the Islamists and the ruling authoritarians view liberal education, the influence of outside ideas and influences, as a threat.

A: A lot of people are trying to escape from Turkey because of the economy, the corruption. The government is doing nothing, it is because of the government.

BG: *What do you mean by corruption?*

A: The president and his party, they are not educated, he does not even have a university education. And you have to have that according to the Constitution. It's a one-man rule now. If you talk about that, you can go to jail. The media is owned by him. The schools. The journalists who write against the government are exiled or flee to avoid prison.

BG: *When reporters speak out strongly what happens?*

A: Jail. Not only reporters. I have a friend on Facebook sued by the Minister of Religion because he called the minister stupid.

BG: *So where is Turkey heading?*

A: Industry does not produce much anymore. We import lentils, we used to grow half the world's lentils. Farming, animal breeding is declining. We were an animal breeding and farming country. Farmers cannot buy gasoline for their tractors. People started hating each other because the government breeds division, you are either with them or with us. Young people do not feel hopeful or appreciated. They want to go abroad. People have lost hope. The fish stinks from the head. We don't have unity; we don't have love for our country.

Gezi Park was like a Gandhi thing. There were gatherings in my town, always peaceful. Even the covered Muslims opened tables for potluck, it was like a festival, they opened a library. Covered, uncovered, Muslim, secular people all together in the name of saving the park. (A wave of demonstrations in Turkey began on May 28, 2013, to protest the development plan for Istanbul's Taksim Gezi Park, then spread nationally. Three and a half million people in an estimated 5,000 demonstrations across Turkey participated, with sometimes violent police reactions.)

I love my country, a most beautiful country, but we don't feel in charge anymore.

Asya asks me about my trip and I walk her through fond memories of trains and meals and landmarks.

A: No, what did people tell you?

BG: *Each country's experience with autocracy is different. If fascism comes to my country, it will be a uniquely American variation.*

⌒

I tell her about Dachau and the Spanish Civil War, of the horrors experienced by my ancestors and other out of favor ethnic or political groups. How ordinary people become indifferent to human suffering. We talk about the idea and obligations of a citizen.

Asya changes the subject to instruct me on the seaside resorts I must visit while in the country. We look at them together on my phone as I calculate whether I can squeeze in a day trip or two, postpone my flight. It's impractical but I like impromptu travel planning. Then I ask if we can meet again, perhaps tomorrow, for a more formal interview here in Kadiköy or even by phone. She demurs, "I have a concert with my girlfriend after work." But there's another reason. She is terrified of being reported. I'm surprised. I didn't get that sense of fear in Budapest, or anywhere on the trip. Her demeanor reminds me that dissent is not tolerated in an increasingly large swath of the world.

It is getting late and we say our goodbyes and swap WhatsApp numbers. It's lonely on the road so the periodic meetup with an old friend or a new stranger eases the sense of isolation. I prefer experiencing local public transport but it's nearing midnight and if I have the Turkish lira exchange rate correct, an Uber is not that costly. I order one and Asya promises to watch for him as I make a dash for the bathroom as the cocktails demand entry into the Istanbul plumbing system.

In the car, the Kurdish driver rails against Erdogan's persecution of his community. I mention my time in Kurdish Iraq and we talk about Sykes-Picot, the disastrous British-French agreement that carved up the Middle East post-WWI. He asks what I had for dinner and I tell him that I enjoyed lahmacun and adana kebab at Adana Ocakbasi restaurant. With conviction, he declares that most popular Turkish dishes are Kurdish.

We cross the Bosporus and bridges are brightly lit in red contrasting with the million lights from Europe's most populous city across the Asia- and Europe-side cityscapes. I'm feeling tired from a long day, still absorbing all I heard tonight. I should rest for my final day and flight home but I hope for at least one final Saturday night encounter with this place.

Southwest across the Sea of Marmara lies another strait, the Dardanelles. There, according to Greek legend, Hero, a virgin priestess of Aphrodite lit a lamp so that the young Leander could—heroically—swim across the strait each night to visit her. One night, the winds are too strong for Hero to light his way and Leander dies in the quickening currents. Hero throws herself to her death in grief. These days, there are more efficient ways to be heroic. Voting would be good. Or supporting better candidates or leadership. Or taking to the streets.

The taxi pulls up in front of the hotel and, as I say goodbye, I hear something strangely familiar from down the street. It's *Bella Ciao*, something of an anthem for me during my travels. Throwing my Osprey over my right shoulder, I run down the cobblestone street toward the source of the music. It's an old hotel with an outdoor restaurant and I take a seat a few tables from the band. The waiter brings a menu but I just order a simple double raki. And sing along for the final stanza.

Someday people will pick the flowers
O bella ciao, bella ciao, bella ciao ciao ciao,
Someday people will pick the flowers
And they will remember me.

This is the flower of resistance
O bella ciao, bella ciao, bella ciao ciao ciao,
This is the flower of resistance
And those who died for liberty.

Acknowledgements

THIS BOOK IS A COLLABORATIVE PROJECT born of a sense of urgency to better understand the nature of fascism in its various forms.

Charlie Evans, Nicole Maron, and Jamie Wrate provided valuable ongoing editorial and research assistance throughout the effort. Charlie took many hours of interviews, transferred in real time from nine countries, and turned them into editable chapter segments, a challenging task. Nicole and Jamie shared insights and perspectives in meetings and calls throughout the year, providing details of country histories as well as quotes and news reports.

Tom Vater is a friend, literary mentor, and top shelf editor, offering cogent advice, political perspective, and good times throughout the process. His intellectual honesty and keen understanding of European political history elevated the conceptual framework and brought the book to completion in its very short time frame.

The book is a gathering of important and diverse voices and I am indebted to the interviewees I met along the way. Some, like Robert Paxton, Adam Hochschild, and Eric Alterman are favorite authors, making the effort a unique privilege. They gave freely of their time, presenting their best thinking on each of their country's political issues. This book contains a good number of the encounters and formal interviews captured along the way. Additional interviews will be shared in future editions and social media platforms in the months ahead. Special thanks to João Paulo Carreteiro for walking me through the Aljube antifascism museum in Lisbon, to Mauro Mello for our Sunday brunch chat overlooking the Targus River, and to Odila Coelho Braga and her friend Diogo for welcoming me to Cascais. Thank to you to, Fernando Coehlo for introducing me to so many who made the first leg of the trip successful. *Forte abraço.*

Alexandru Oprescu is a long-time publishing colleague who designed the book's interior and exterior and prepared it for publication. He is fast, thoughtful, skilled, and highly sensitive to a book's creative needs.

This is my third literary project funded via the Kickstarter crowdfunding platform. The initial campaign achieved its goal in only two weeks. Crowdfunding is not just about the money, it is a process of validation, support, and community building that helps inform and direct a creative effort. Thanks to all 60 supporters, and to those who stepped up to higher levels of patronage allowing the project to proceed, people like "Producers" Lou Borrelli and Bill O'Luanaigh, and "Patrons" Spencer Nassar, Derek Brown, Evan Shatz, Joan Cainan, Kate Donohue, Chaun Muir, Bill Cobham, Rochelle Kopp and Steven Ganz, Deborah Denney, Steven Herman, Pat Reilly, and Adam Edwards.

Many friends provided the encouragement and ongoing moral support that made this journey possible. It was a long haul across Europe in four weeks, and old and new friends bucked me up and provided the good humor and confidence needed during solitary moments.

As with all these projects, the kindness of strangers made it all that much easier and memorable. The hotel receptionists who allowed an early morning check-in, the waiters and train staff and museum guides and hundred serendipitous encounters that turned a mad dash across Europe into a peak experience.

Thanks to all who contributed in large and small ways to make this possible.

And, finally, thank you Andrea, Justin, Silas, and Cecelia for your loving care, allowing me to get mind and body ready for my cross-continent jaunt.

About the Author

Born in Brooklyn, New York, Brian Gruber spent 40 years studying, leading, and developing new media companies and creative projects. Hired by C-SPAN founder Brian Lamb to be the pioneering cable network's first head of marketing, he hosted two weekly national call-in shows interviewing prominent guests such as John McCain, Nancy Pelosi, and Cesar Chavez. After years as a cable TV marketing turnaround specialist, he was hired as the first head of marketing for Australia's national cable television company FOXTEL.

While consulting for the World Affairs Council, Brian founded FORA.tv, a global thought leader network presenting the world's leading public forums; it was named by *Time* magazine as one of the fifty best sites on the web. While there, he interviewed numerous intellectuals, writers, and policy experts, from Christopher Hitchens and Norman Mailer to Malcolm Gladwell and Jim Lehrer. He also founded ShowGo.tv, which streamed live concerts from iconic jazz clubs in Brazil, the UK, Italy, and the United States.

Since leaving the startup world, Brian has published five books with travel themes.

Dauphin, Dorian and Dead: The Year Without a Net is a tragicomic romp through four continents that explores the ascent, descent, and aftermath of romance in midlife.

WAR: The Afterparty is a global "walkabout" to the scenes of a half century of U.S. military interventions. In addition to interviews on Fox News, C-SPAN, and public radio, the book was widely praised in reviews for its vision and editorial style. Stephen Kinzer, former *New York Times* bureau chief and one of America's leading foreign policy authors, commented, "Joining the army, according to an old proverb, gives you the chance to 'travel the world, meet interesting people, and kill them.' In this book, Brian Gruber travels the world, meets extremely interesting people, and instead of killing them, tries to understand them. His book cuts through layers of propaganda and helps us see the world's problems—and ourselves—through the eyes of others."

Six Days at Ronnie Scott's: Billy Cobham on Jazz Fusion and the Act of Creation garnered rave reviews across the jazz community. Carlo Wolff of *Downbeat* called it, "… an unusual and welcome addition to the jazz bibliography." Geoff Nicholls of *Rhythm* magazine adds, "Well-written and thought-provoking… a challenging document of a half-century of cutting-edge musical exploration."

Surmountable: How Citizens from Selma to Seoul Changed the World chronicles the victories and setbacks of ten American and three international citizen movements from the past century. Co-written with Adam Monier Edwards, Brian Gruber traveled across the United States and four continents to gather stories from activists, journalists, and witnesses from sites of groundbreaking protests. What was the original vision for citizen engagement of Enlightenment thinkers that inspired U.S. liberal democracy and how do we move mountains to create the kind of world we want?

Full Moon over Koh Phangan explores the Thai island's characters, communities, and magnetic appeal. What attracts Phangan's eclectic range of adventurers? What makes the island so uniquely interesting and attractive to visitors seeking a new life, transcendence, restoration or, simply, a memorable, gorgeous respite from the world? An eclectic range of longtime residents share their answers to those questions.